Praise for The Bu

"Michael Jacobsen's book is packed with practical advice and addresses – everything a creative sector entrepreneur needs to know to run and grow their business successfully. Highly recommended!"

Luka Blackman-Gibbs, NACUE Create manager

"The Business of Creativity *is a must-read for any aspiring creative or digital media entrepreneur. It is a practical resource encapsulating years of experience which I thoroughly recommend to you if you want to run a business in these sectors.*"

Jon Bradford, managing director, TechStars

"A great guide for anyone thinking about embarking on their entrepreneurial journey. The lessons and examples here are valuable to creative and non-creative propositions alike. If you're considering starting a business, or if you're already in the middle of doing it, you should read Michael Jacobsen's book before you make your next decision!"

Andrew Humphries, co-founder, The Bakery London and UKTI Dealmaker

"With The Business of Creativity *Michael has produced a brilliant overview of all of the issues around building a successful enterprise in the creative sectors. With practical resources, interesting case studies and real-life advice, this book should be a must read for creative, media and digital media entrepreneurs.*"

Ian Merricks, managing partner, White Horse Capital LLP

"Michael Jacobsen is a creative entrepreneur who has been there and done it. He knows what it takes to make it in this sector and in this insightful guide he draws on the benefit of his experience to point aspiring creatives in the right direction. I recommend it."

Doug Richard, founder, School for Creative Startups

"As a serial entrepreneur, Michael delivers a refreshingly creative and practical take on the essentials of starting and running a business."

Guy Rigby, entrepreneur, business enthusiast and author of 'From Vision to Exit: The Entrepreneur's Guide to Building and Selling a Business'

"The market is saturated with books giving advice to prospective entrepreneurs whereas The Business of Creativity *is probably unique in targeting the creative sector. I know Michael, his success speaks for itself, and his voice is so clearly heard throughout this book. Amazingly he has produced a working tool for creatives intending to build a business but equally cleverly his advice applies to all who want the inside know-how on how this can be successfully achieved."*

Michael Vine, Founder, Objective Productions and manager, Derren Brown

"Michael Jacobsen is a great entrepreneur and has made a substantial contribution to the British creative sector. The Business of Creativity *shows his commitment to nurturing and mentoring entrepreneurs, and provides very valuable and wise counsel to those in the creative sector. Given the highly valuable experience and advice it combines, I thoroughly recommend it as essential reading and a must-have resource."*

Eric Woollard-White, board member, Peter Jones Foundation and founder, Thirty7 Productions

THE BUSINESS OF
CREATIVITY

AN EXPERT GUIDE TO STARTING AND GROWING A BUSINESS IN THE CREATIVE SECTOR

BY MICHAEL JACOBSEN

HARRIMAN HOUSE LTD
3A Penns Road
Petersfield
Hampshire
GU32 2EW
GREAT BRITAIN

Tel: +44 (0)1730 233870
Email: enquiries@harriman-house.com
Website: www.harriman-house.com

First published in Great Britain in 2013.

ISBN: 9781908003362

British Library Cataloguing in Publication Data
A CIP catalogue record for this book can be obtained from the British Library.

Printed and bound in Great Britain by
Marston Book Services Limited, Oxfordshire

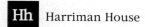 Harriman House

For Melvyn

eBook edition

As a buyer of the print edition of *The Business of Creativity* you can now download the eBook edition free of charge to read on an eBook reader, your smartphone or your computer. Simply go to:

http://ebooks.harriman-house.com/businessofcreativityebook

or point your smartphone at the QRC below.

You can then register and download your free eBook.

www.harriman-house.com

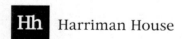 Harriman House

CONTENTS

ABOUT THE AUTHOR

MICHAEL JACOBSEN is an Australian-born serial entrepreneur, now based in Europe. He holds a Bachelor of Business degree from UTS in Sydney and a financial diploma from the Australian Securities Institute. He is active in UK and European business and is also an angel investor and business mentor to start ups, growth businesses and businesses in the creative sector, predominantly in the UK and Europe. He sits on the board of the world-renowned Australian Centre for Event Management, a division of the business faculty at the University of Technology Sydney.

Michael co-founded/owned and was founding co-producer of *Dirty Dancing – The Classic story on Stage*, which held its world premiere in Australia in 2004 and has since played in Holland, Canada, the USA, Germany and London's West End. It set box office records in Germany, Canada and London and is one of the most successful live entertainment products ever staged in terms of ticket sales and revenue.

Michael also co-founded and developed the 13,000-seat Vector Arena in Auckland, New Zealand, and sat on the board as an executive director. For a number of years he was also on the board of the 2000-seat Capitol Theatre in Sydney and was CEO and board member of the 12,000-seat Sydney Entertainment Centre for six years. He has also been involved in the promotion of concert tours by numerous leading artists including Elton John, Bruce Springsteen and Barbra Streisand.

Alongside his own entrepreneurial activities, Michael is active as a business mentor in the UK and Europe. He has taken numerous companies to market and worked with others on how to become investable – assisting them in gaining finance, venture capital and private equity.

Michael is passionate about education and in addition to his work as a business mentor, he lectures at universities in London, is a mentor at the Peter Jones Enterprise Academy, sits on the steering committee for NACUE Create (National Association of College and University Entrepreneurs), has acted as a resident entrepreneur for the StartUp Britain campaign and is a mentor for the Doug Richard School for Creative Startups.

With thanks to

My family, Emma Jones, Myles Hunt, Dr Usama Jannoun, Paul Manley, Ben Posen, Kamran Bedai, Scott Russell Hill and Lord Archer

PREFACE

THE CREATIVE SECTOR forms a large part of the British and European economy, encompassing the following areas:

- Advertising
- Architecture
- Arts and antique markets
- Crafts
- Design
- Designer fashion
- Film, video and photography
- Musical and visual performing arts
- Publishing
- Radio
- Software, computer games and electronic publishing
- Television

Business and creativity will always be an uneasy marriage, but it is a marriage of convenience and also a marriage of necessity.

With this book I want to empower and equip those who have creative passion, who have launched creative start ups and those who are growing creative businesses with the specialist knowledge I have gained from my experience as a creative entrepreneur. I also want to inspire the millions of people employed in creative industries in Britain and Europe to start their own businesses.

Drawing on my own experience, lessons I have learned, and what I have seen to work and to fail in my own businesses and those I have invested in or mentored, I have put together this easy-to-digest business book.

You don't have to read it from front to back (but you can if you want!) It is arranged sequentially, taking you through the various stages of the business journey from start up, to growth, to the pressing question of what to do next when you close the book.

I do not hold myself up to be flawless, in fact I have tried to draw on my own successes and failures to impart knowledge to you. All entrepreneurs have their fair share of both, but the important thing is to come out on top.

I am fortunate to have had more successes than failures and I put that down to learning from mistakes and learning from others. You only come out on top through learning and education, and using this to add more value, and to create and implement better systems. This is good business. You won't win every race, but pace yourself, train and win as many gold medals as you can.

A last point to note here is that throughout the book I have included *spotlight* case studies of some of Britain's best creative sector companies. These are headed up by entrepreneurs who have a passion for their particular art form, and who have built a successful business around that. These should provide you with inspiration!

Use this book to regularly acquaint yourself with the tools you need to turn your creative passion into a viable, successful, long-term business.

INTRODUCTION

A passion for business

FROM THE TIME I WAS YOUNG all I ever wanted to do was be in business. My father was in business and from the age of five I used to go to his office with him on weekends or during holidays and sit there going through papers on his desk. My parents even bought me a little briefcase!

Through school the idea of holding a job down never appealed to me and when I was at university studying business I did not think about what job I might be able to get from it, but rather how I could apply the knowledge I was gaining to start and run my own business.

My interest in business was piqued at school when I was fortunate enough to have a wealthy commerce teacher who was already a successful stock market trader. I would often arrive early for class and he would talk about what he was investing in and explain how he chose the stocks, recommending certain books I could read for research (it was pre-internet days... but only just).

So I started trading while I was still at school, aged 16. After some initial success I realised that making money was fun and the activity of business itself was even more enjoyable than I had thought it would be. I realised that if I traded successfully and built up a bank of funds then I could invest that money into business and property, thereby not only generating cash flow but also growing my assets and putting money away safely.

Having finished university I got a job in stock broking with a bank. The worst part about this was that I was restricted in what I could trade myself. I also started to build up a property portfolio. One of my best friends was in property development and we would have endless coffees whilst he explained to me how the property market worked at a commercial level.

Creative business

The undertone to all of this was that my family's business was in entertainment. I did not necessarily want to be in business with them, although entertainment was in my blood because I had been exposed to showbiz from the time I was born. I was very happy with the stock broking world; I was financially secure and enjoyed success in property, stock and derivative trading.

Eventually opportunities arose where I could do both, so in addition to my own businesses I became a shareholder in my family's business. After several years of ups and downs, successes and failures, litigation and love, we turned the company from a *fee for service* business, promoting and producing shows, into a property owner and manager, developing arenas and entertainment venues, and owning the intellectual property rights to shows. The most notable of these was the theatrical production *Dirty Dancing – The Classic Story On Stage*, to which we owned the world rights.

I co-owned and was founding co-producer of *Dirty Dancing*, which held its world premiere in Australia in 2004. This production has since played in Holland, Canada, America, Germany and London's West End. *Dirty Dancing* set box office records in Germany and London. With sold out performances and a global gross to date in excess of US$500m, it is regarded as one of the most successful musicals of all time, alongside *Phantom of the Opera*, *Miss Saigon*, *Mamma Mia* and *Cats*. It became a global phenomenon and was valued at over US$100m when I exited.

Over the past decade I have been involved in concert promotion, theatrical production and rights ownership, venue management and ownership and development, as well as angel investing. This work has included taking numerous companies to market, counselling them on how to become investable and then helping them to gain finance, venture capital and private equity. I have also been involved with property development, public speaking, mentoring and co-founding companies across a variety of sectors.

I also co-founded and co-developed the 13,000-seat *Vector Arena* (the Auckland Entertainment Centre) in Auckland, New Zealand. I have been chairman of what is arguably Australasia's leading theatre, the 2000-seat Capitol Theatre in Sydney, and also of the 11,000-seat Sydney Entertainment Centre, winner of multiple global awards as *entertainment venue of the year.*

I left these positions after a sale process to exit them and monetise the investments was set in motion . The Sydney Entertainment Centre, for example, was revalued three years after opening and had produced a 300% ROI.

Creative sector businesses remain my passion and my role has always been on the business side; the *business* of creativity is *my thing*!

A move into mentoring

In the years following my move to Europe I have not worked full time. I now undertake philanthropic work at the Peter Jones Foundation and Doug Richard's School for Creative Startups. I am on the steering committee for NACUE/Create (National Association of College & University Entrepreneurs) and sit on the board of the Australian Centre for Event Management, a subsidiary of the Faculty of Business at Sydney's University of Technology (UTS).

I have also lectured at the University of Westminster and for UK Trade and Investment (UKTI). I was a founding mentor at the Accelerator Academy in London and I act as a mentor for Springboard, the UK and European Accelerator. Commercially, I established a company to mentor entrepreneurs.

I do this mentoring work because I enjoy it and because I noticed that most mentoring was being done either by salesmen or by people who were just teachers of theory and had no practical experience of actually starting or running a business.

When business and creativity collide

One thing I have witnessed is that creative entrepreneurs generally fall into two categories: those who keep a day job and do their creative work on the side, perhaps as a hobby, and sometimes receive a small income from it but only on a spare change scale; and those who want to take their concept to a commercial level.

To many in the creative sector, *money*, *cash* and *profit* are dirty words. To many in the commercial world the creative sector is not taken seriously as a business. A creative business left to creative people alone will have no business direction. Likewise, a creative business left to business people alone will have no creative streak.

These stereotypes are changing and creative sector entrepreneurs are realising that they can turn their passion into a business and keep its creative integrity, if they structure their enterprise correctly. Similarly, many in business now view the creative sector as a serious proposition with growth potential, in addition to it being a contribution to UK culture.

Even the British government recognises this and is placing the creative sector as a commercial sector firmly on its agenda. The EU is similarly placing importance on it, releasing policy papers and injecting funds into the European Creative Community.

Given these facts and the position I have come from, firstly in traditional business and later amalgamating my financial and business expertise with my creative passion, I work actively to bring these two camps together and to help creative entrepreneurs realise their passion. When this happens the creative person can afford to do what they love every day for the rest of their lives. What better way is there to live than that?

My intention in writing this book is to help start ups and creative sector entrepreneurs receive a business education so they can structure their endeavours appropriately and so theirs can become a viable business.

I hope that you enjoy the book and find it to be useful.

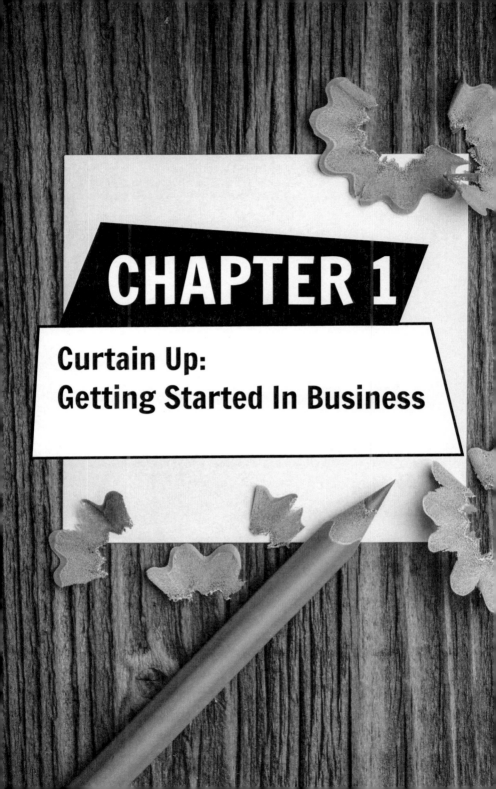

CHAPTER 1

Curtain Up:
Getting Started In Business

THE INGREDIENTS FOR SUCCESS

ONE OF THE THINGS I am constantly witnessing is how obscure the path seems to be for entrepreneurs wanting to get into business in the creative industries. It is often opaque at best. Many creative entrepreneurs therefore understandably struggle to work out where to begin when aiming to turn their burning passion into a commercial start up.

As a consultant and mentor for creative sector businesses and entrepreneurs this is the No. 1 question I see from creative start ups – "Where do I start?" The other two key issues I see are concerns over finance ("I don't have any money, I can't start a business!") and an overall lack of knowledge about business structure.

Creative sector businesses are unique in that often they are synonymous with their founder. Look at Sir Paul Smith and his eponymous fashion chain; *The X Factor* and Simon Cowell are inextricably linked; and where the man Steven Spielberg and the brand Steven Spielberg diverge is impossible to tell.

For this reason, it is more important than ever to ensure good business principles are enshrined. In that way the entrepreneur can be the person *and* the commercial business. If you don't do this, you will always own a job, not a business.

So, having a clear **vision** and **mission** is the key starting point.

I have put together a full checklist for you to look at and refer to as often as you can, to ensure that you are laying the foundation for your creative business from day one. See how would you rate your own feelings on each one of these.

Checklist of ingredients for success

1. A clear **vision** for the company.

2. A clear **mission** (how you are going to implement your vision).

3. A clear set of **values** (this underscores the integrity of your brand).

4. A clear plan for the next **120 days** laying out what you need to do day by day to get your business into shape. Make a brain dump and put timings around it with milestones. Easy!

5. Engage with a **coach, mentor** or good friend who has business savvy. Someone you can bounce ideas off and who can elevate you. This is what works for athletes and performers.

6. Know who **your customer** is and what needs they have that your business will fulfil. For example, if you are a jazz singer looking to do backing vocals, you are a freelancer and your customers may be TV producers, session bands or even touring bands who are auditioning backing singers.

7. Know your **unique selling point (USP)**. With creative businesses, the USP is often the very gift or skill of the creative individual: the singing skills (talent) of the freelance backing singer; the sculpting skills (talent) of the craft store owner; or the graphic and design skills (talent) of the small production house owner.

    USP is not just a unique selling point, however. USP is hooked into the need of your customer.

    Charles Revson, the legendary founder of the Revlon makeup company, said his **USP** was *hope*. He believed he was selling *hope*, rather than products, that would make his customers beautiful. Think about this and the oblique but smart logic behind his thoughts.

8. Understand **basic marketing** and how this is relevant to your offering. So, for example, if you are a videographer looking to freelance at weddings is your marketing just word of mouth?

No! Marketing is your product, that is the quality of your work; the price you charge; how you deliver yourself; and promotion. It is **product, price, place and promotion** – the **4 Ps**. Understand them and base your marketing plan around them. It is a common misconception that marketing is only promotion.

9. Have an understanding of **basic business structure.** If you are a freelancer, are you a company or a sole trader? Are you registered for VAT or do you fall below the threshold?

If you set up a quick and easy structure now it could cause you problems later as the business launches on a growth trajectory.

The creative sector is full of freelancers and small businesses, so sole traders are common, but you need advice on what structure fits you, your goal and your personal circumstances. This may make your eyes glaze over, but it is integral to ensuring your business is structured for commercial protection and success.

10. **Financials**. You need an understanding of how you are going to make money if you are looking to commercialise your creativity. You don't need to be a financial expert as there are many resources available to help you. We will cover this in greater detail later.

*

Run through the list and see how much progress you can make. If you address each of the points above, you will have a sufficient **business plan** to make a start.

A SOUND FOOTING FOR YOUR BUSINESS

How do you put your business on the right footing for growth from the very beginning, to give yourself the best chance of becoming that next great creative entrepreneur? How do you become the Simon Cowell, Sir Paul Smith or Sir Terence Conran of your niche?

There are three key prerequisites to growing your start up creative business from day 1 that don't involve balance sheets, business plans or complex modelling systems. I will look at these now.

1. Have courage in your vision

I repeatedly find the same things lacking in companies that are struggling to grow; it is a psychological impediment related to a lack of courage. From our early lives, there is a lot of negativity surrounding feelings of uncertainty or being mistaken about something. We then lack the courage to attempt new or unusual ventures. This leads to a collective, subconscious lack of courage in society, resulting in an anxiety that prevents individuals from starting businesses, or holding back their growth if they do.

You need to have a belief in your **vision**. If you don't even have a vision yet, you don't have anything to believe in. So you need one.

We all know people who are going to start a business *one day*, marketing their crafts or putting their videographer skills into commercial practice at weddings and functions, but they never do. They are talkers, but they lack courage. They also lack clarity. I happen to believe that never starting is more of a failure than starting and falling short.

Did Simon Cowell lack the courage to rebuild a business when he was broke 15 years ago and had to move back in with his parents? No. He had the courage to start again and build the empire he presides over today.

So write down your **vision** – your **foundation** – own it, and espouse it everywhere you go. This **vision** brings you clarity and manifests your dream day by day, giving you courage that this is not just a dream but a real business concept and a potentially commercial reality.

2. Assess the need

I often read questions such as "What is the magic formula for knowing if my product or creative business concept will be a success?"

This can be addressed by asking "What is the need?" and "Do you have the desire and the heart to serve that need?"

If there is no immediate or visible need for your product, that doesn't necessarily preclude it. Ten years ago who knew we needed iPhones and iPads? No one except Steve Jobs who, as we know, saw the need and made people realise they had that need. He educated through clever marketing that tapped into basic desires.

Do you want to serve a need?

Do you know what need you are serving?

If you answer yes to both, you have a solid business foundation.

3. Coach, mentor or friend

Most successful creative sector entrepreneurs have someone to engage with, someone who they bounce ideas off and from whom they can obtain an objective opinion. It's what all successful people in the world do, across all fields, not only the creative sector.

Who has ever heard of an athlete winning a race without a coach or training, or an actor in Hollywood or on the West End stage without a director and a team beside him or her, and who doesn't do rehearsals?

Success doesn't come in those fields without mentoring, coaching and support, and it won't come without them in business either. You need a mentor who can provide you with clear, objective counsel and train your business skills and personal mindset.

Businesses are spoilt for choice in the UK as there are so many places to turn for help. Whatever your budget, even if it is nonexistent, there is help in the form of mentors and coaches, and even objective family and friends.

Obtaining advice and filling the gaps in your own knowledge strengthens your mindset and business skill base. Strengthening your mindset and business skill base trains you for success.

Thirty7 Productions

Thirty7 Productions is an independent theatre, film and media production company headquartered in London, with production offices in Cardiff and Los Angeles. Its focus is primarily theatre and film projects, and television production.

Owned by Scot Williams and Eric Woollard-White, Thirty7 benefits from Scot and Eric's network of contacts and experience, built up over 40-plus years of collective working in film, theatre, television and business. This puts the company in a strong position financially, with good access to investment and excellent relations with studios, theatre and broadcasters.

Thirty7 is unique as there are few truly independent boutique production companies in the UK. Being such a company allows Thirty7 to take on projects which are creative, edgy and make a valuable contribution to the creative industries.

www.thirty7productions.com

Alyssa Smith Jewellery

ALYSSA SMITH IS A 26-YEAR-OLD jewellery designer from Hertfordshire. In the past year her company has been a finalist for or won over 15 national business or accessories awards. It is also a favourite jeweller to the stars as Dawn Porter, Suzi Perry, Caroline Flack, Emma Kennedy, Gail Porter, Sienna Miller and Jason Bradbury have all appeared on and off the screen wearing Alyssa's creations.

Alyssa's handcrafted work has been hailed by countless publications, including the *Guardian*, the *Sunday Express* and *Bride* magazine. In the March 2012 issue *Start Your Business* magazine she was named alongside Facebook's Mark Zuckerberg as one of the top 20 young entrepreneurs worldwide.

Alyssa is a great example of a growth entrepreneur because she has achieved these global and celebrity accolades from her studio in Hertfordshire where she works alone to supply her worldwide demand.

This is a perfect example of *doing it from your spare room*. What an amazing creative sector entrepreneur!

www.alyssasmith.co.uk

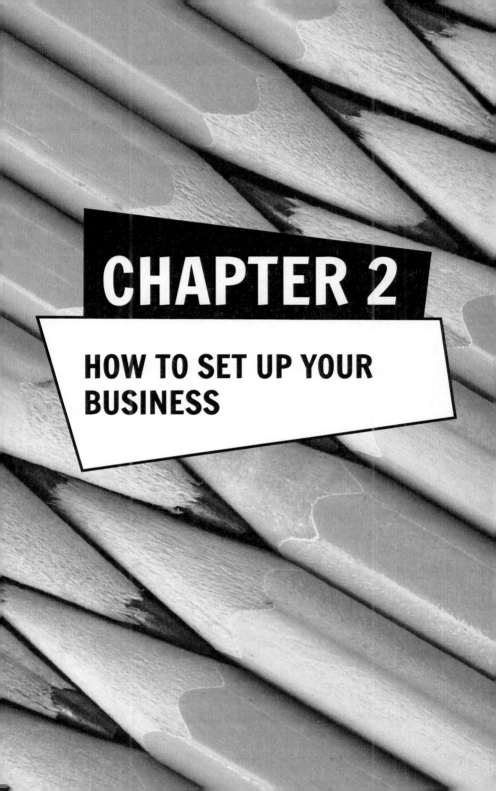

CHAPTER 2

HOW TO SET UP YOUR BUSINESS

SETTING UP YOUR BUSINESS IS IMPORTANT. In my experience as an entrepreneur, investor and mentor, the most fatal mistakes are made at the beginning. I'm not saying entrepreneurs need to adopt an administrative, managerial attitude to business. What I know is that there are some clear steps to get your head around early on that will set you up in the best way structurally, mentally and financially.

There are many decisions which people just aren't aware are milestones, such as setting the vision; deciding to buy a business or simply setting up a new one; determining the optimal business structure; and deducing if there is one business system that will allow you to operate more efficiently and profitably than another.

Many entrepreneurs erroneously believe you start a business by coming up with an idea, writing a business plan and then raising money. To me, this misses the most important steps for long-term strength, support and growth. It is these steps that I have outlined in this chapter.

VISION, MISSION AND VALUES

Vision, mission and values statements are key learning in any business degree. Big businesses are also the greatest exponents of these methods. Most start up and growth businesses I speak to have never heard of them, or believe they are a waste of time and thought.

I see it differently – vision, mission and values statements are vital tools which form the foundation for your whole organisation, forever.

Vision statement

Business is a journey and, like a road trip, a drive made without a map or SatNav would be asking to take the scenic route. In business, the scenic route is not desirable; if you want to take that route you are best keeping your creative passion as a hobby.

To ensure you are not heading out on the journey blind, you need a vision statement – this tells you and everyone else where you business is going. The purpose of a vision statement is precisely what it says on the tin – to set your course for the journey ahead.

It is easy setting a vision statement; just dream up where you want your organisation to go – imagine where you would go if there were no restrictions or obstacles; if you really could be the best you wanted to be – and write it down! A good statement is a paragraph, or just two brief sentences, which is positive and inspirational. It should be reviewed every three to five years, or when the vision has been achieved.

The vision statement can be a public or a private piece of work. Bigger brands will tend to make theirs public whilst smaller companies may keep it in their office or taped to the computer as a reminder of where they want to go. Investors love vision statements as it gives them greater confidence. After all, who would invest in a company without a vision?

So, to keep you, your employees and your stakeholders focused, a vision statement is imperative.

I am surprised by how many people think of this as *wishy washy* and do not recognise its significance. As further evidence, take a look at some famous brands and their vision statements.

Vision statements of famous brands

Avon

To be the company that best understands and satisfies the product, service and self-fulfilment needs of women – globally.

Nike

1960s: *Crush Adidas*

Current: *To be the number one athletic company in the world*

Brighton and Hove City Council - Music and Arts

Our vision is for all children and young people in the city, whatever their background, to be able to engage with, to enjoy, and to be inspired by high quality music and arts opportunities.

Disney

We create happiness by providing the finest in entertainment for people of all ages, everywhere.

BBC

To be the most creative organisation in the world.

McDonald's

McDonald's vision is to be the world's best quick service restaurant experience. Being the best means providing outstanding quality, service, cleanliness, and value, so that we make every customer in every restaurant smile.

Toys R Us

To put joy in kids' hearts and a smile on parents' faces.

Kraft Foods

Helping People around the World Eat and Live Better.

Mission statement

Where the vision statement is the creation of a dream and a statement of intent, a *mission statement* is more down to earth and provides the path of how you are going to get where the vision demands you go. Basically the mission statement explains how you are going to get there.

"A mission statement helps clarify what business you are in, your goals and your objectives," says Rhonda Abrams, author of *The Successful Business Plan: Secrets and Strategies*.

Once again, the mission statement is also an important tool to guide stakeholders and is often used publicly in the same manner as the vision statement.

A useful brainstorm to help devise your mission is to answer these questions:

- Why are you in business?
- Who are your customers?
- What image of your business do you want to convey?
- What is the nature of your products and services?
- What level of service do you provide?
- What roles do you and your employees play?
- What kind of relationships will you maintain with suppliers?
- How do you differ from your competitors?
- How will you use technology, capital, processes, products and services to reach your goals?
- What underlying philosophies or values guided your responses to the previous questions?

Some of the leading companies in the FTSE 100 have mission statements, as do some of the world's leading brands. Here are a few examples.

Example mission statements

Starbucks

To inspire and nurture the human spirit – one person, one cup and one neighbourhood at a time.

Saatchi & Saatchi

Our mission is to be revered as the hothouse for world changing ideas.

Coca-Cola

To refresh the world – in mind, body and spirit

To inspire moments of optimism – through our brands and actions

To create value and make a difference everywhere we engage

BBC

To enrich people's lives with programmes and services that inform, educate and entertain.

Tesco

Creating value for customers, to earn their lifetime loyalty.

eBay

We help people trade practically anything on earth

Google

To organise the world's information and make it universally accessible and useful

Classy Tickets

Classy Tickets' mission is very simple: we are striving to be the best online source for buying tickets to entertainment events. To attain this we will attempt to do whatever it takes to distinguish ourselves from the competition and to leave our customers satisfied. This means the best price and the best customer service and follow up. If at any time we do not achieve this, please take the time to let us know what we can do better.

Topshop

Topshop is considered to be the ultimate pioneer of high street fashion in London, gaining much popularity over the last decade. Our first American shop was launched in Soho, New York City, last year. That marked the start of our international journey, and soon we will have stores in China, Japan, Korea and other high fashioned Asian countries. Topshop is committed to delivering runway fashion to everyone on the street by expanding our worldwide market.

Jamie Oliver

Anyone can learn to cook... it's fun, cool, can save you money and help you, your family and friends to live a healthier life.

James Dyson

Take everyday products that don't work well, and make them work better.

Values statement

An often overlooked element of structuring a business is a *values statement*. I always tell people to write one.

A values statement is an expression of a company's or individual's core beliefs. Companies write the statement to connect with the consumer. Additionally, the declaration allows for the company's staff to be aware of the priorities and goals of the company. For example, a company might list one of its guiding principles as "Customer service is priority one."

The values statement, along with the vision and mission statements, will form the culture of a company. It communicates to your stakeholders, your clients and customers what you are all about and what your business stands for.

Core values are traits or qualities that you consider not just worthwhile; they represent an individual's or organisation's highest priorities, deeply held beliefs and fundamental driving forces. Core values define what your organisation believes and how you want your organisation to resonate with and appeal to employees and the external world.

The values statement acts as a corporate conscience, guiding everyone in the organisation at all times, and allowing every person inside the company and every person you deal with to be infused with your heart and mindset at all times, especially at times when access to you as the founder of the business may be difficult.

Going further, a values statement will allow everything to be created in your image and will allow your image to be woven into the company's image. Moving forward, everyone will have a reference point as well as a guiding light if ever they question what to do in a particular situation.

A good example of this is the US Constitution. Created in the image of the Founding Fathers, it guides US politicians and the American public towards what decisions to take and what America stands for.

So it is now no longer what the Founding Fathers stood for, but what America stands for.

In a financial sense, intangible elements which bind and elevate the company (like vision, mission and values) contribute to the *goodwill* of the company, which basically means the company is worth more if and when you sell it.

A good values statement:

- Should create interest

- Contains a value proposition

- Differentiates your offer from your competitor's offer and creates a strong differential between you and your competitors

- Increases the quantity and quality of your sales

- Wins your business greater market share

- Focuses on your customers' hearts and minds

Let's look at the values statements of some large companies.

Values statements of large companies

Microsoft

As a company, and as individuals, we value integrity, honesty, openness, personal excellence, constructive self-criticism, continual self-improvement, and mutual respect. We are committed to our customers and partners and have a passion for technology. We take on big challenges, and pride ourselves on seeing them through. We hold ourselves accountable to our customers, shareholders, partners, and employees by honoring our commitments, providing results, and striving for the highest quality.

Google

Google calls its values and value statements its *philosophy* and they re-look at the components every few years to make sure that the values are still current.

Focus on the user and all else will follow.

It's best to do one thing really, really well.

Fast is better than slow.

Marriott

We believe our strength is rooted in our core values: putting people first, pursuing excellence, embracing change, acting with integrity and serving our world. These values are our legacy and our future. As we pursue our vision of making Marriott the #1 hospitality company in the world, we never lose sight of our founding principles and our proud heritage. Our business is always evolving… but we'll always stay true to who we are.

PayPal

Security has been core value number one at PayPal since its early days, when rampant fraud threatened to bankrupt the company even as it was turning substantial profits. Today, PayPal continues to place supreme importance on providing a safe service for its users and their transactions. Credit card holders, for instance, receive prompt phone calls from PayPal if their cards are charged an abnormally high number of times (or used at a wide range of places) within a single day.

Those wishing to transfer more than $500 per month from PayPal to outside bank accounts are subjected to rigorous screening, including mailing photocopies of their driver's licence, Social Security card and pay stubs to PayPal's fraud division in Nebraska. These and other security measures have their origins in PayPal's beginnings, which remain an ever-present reminder to prioritise security above all else.

Craigslist

Craigslist CEO Jim Buckmaster self-runs his company in the image of his personal values. Craigslist is as anti-corporate as any start up can be. Speaking about eBay's 25% stake in the company, Buckmaster revealed that he only agreed to it on the condition that eBay had no interest in being involved in running the business. He also defended Craigslist's long-standing policy of not running text ads on the grounds that "users haven't asked for them yet."

Indeed, Buckmaster went so far as to explicitly declare that Craigslist "is not trying to maximize revenue."

This might seem strange commercially but it's a great example of the company reflecting the founder's personal values.

Dirty Dancing theatrical production

Here are *Dirty Dancing*'s vision and mission:

Vision

To produce the most successful and profitable stage show the world has ever seen.

Mission

Through the use of the world's best creative team, the careful and strategic selection of partners and co-producers, constant attention to the brand and stability of management, we will create and maintain the most successful, unique and profitable stage show in the world.

GENERAL ADMIN AND TAX (THE BORING STUFF)

Getting your administration right from the start is integral to the success of your business. Regardless of whether you are working from home, an office or a studio, having your affairs in order will assist your business, its growth and your propensity to engage investment. It is a guarantee that this is not as exciting as your business. However, without a solid foundation in this area your business will be unsupported.

Many creative sector entrepreneurs that I have encountered are like myself and dislike this element of business more than most, as it seems to be the antithesis of the imagination-fuelled enterprise we have a passion for. In this case, where appropriate and viable, it is often best to outsource the work to contractors to ensure that it is accurately taken care of.

I have provided a checklist below of some of the crucial areas you need to pay attention to.

VAT

VAT is a tax that is charged on most goods and services that businesses provide in the UK. It is also charged on goods and some services that are imported from countries outside the European Union (EU), and brought into the UK from other EU countries.

VAT is charged when a VAT-registered business sells to either another business or to a non-business customer. When a VAT-registered businesses buy goods or services they can generally reclaim the VAT they've paid.

If you are a business and the goods or services you provide count as what's known as *taxable supplies* you will have to register for VAT if either:

- your turnover for the previous 12 months has gone over a specific limit – called the VAT threshold (currently £79,000)
- you think your turnover will soon go over this limit

You can choose to register for VAT if you want, even if you don't have to. Visit Her Majesty's Revenue & Customs (HMRC) website (**www.hmrc.gov.uk/vat**) to get precise information.

Income taxes

These are direct taxes paid by you or your business on money you earn or capital you gain. In the 2013-14 tax year these are:

- Capital gains tax: 18% (up to £35,000) and 28% (above £35,000)
- Corporation tax: 23%
- Income tax: 20% on earnings £0 to £32,010; 40% on £32,011 to £150,000; 45% over £150,000

National Insurance

This is paid by both the employee and the employer on a scaling basis. You can find more detailed information on your specific sector on the HMRC website (**www.hmrc.gov.uk/ni**).

Business insurance

If you are in business you will need insurance; without it your livelihood is at risk as an unexpected loss could cause financial hardship and destroy years of hard work. Some types of insurance are compulsory by law.

Types of insurance areas to consider are:

- Life/key man insurance
- Household insurance
- Professional insurance
- General business insurance

You need to ensure that if your business is run from home you are properly covered as most polices do not automatically *onceover* you and any employees.

Also make sure if you are going to other people's places, for example if you are a freelancer, that you are covered by their policies. If you are a photographer at a wedding and fall over – who is covering you? Sometimes it will be your responsibility if you are there on business.

Insurance is specialised and you are best to find a reliable insurance broker to advise you. You can find information on the British Insurance Brokers' Association website (**www.biba.org.uk**).

Accounts payable and receivables

Make sure you have a good system for regularly updating your receivables and payables. If you raise invoices make sure your purchasers know the terms. If people pay you late or you have a lot of bad debts, it can kill your cash flow. Many businesses have gone to the wall with a lot of revenue but little of it collected and in their account.

MYOB (**www.myob.com**) is a great system to help you keep on top of this aspect of the business.

Credit with suppliers

Ensure you adhere to all payment terms with suppliers.

Building good credit with suppliers is key for your business relationships and your future cash flow. Just make sure you negotiate good terms with them and pay on time, or a day or two early. If ever you are going to be late, tell them.

RESEARCH

Research is a vital component of starting a business. The technical term for research in the business world is *due diligence*.

As the saying goes: "If you fail to plan you plan to fail." If you want to lay a solid foundation, research all the key areas you will need to know about in the first few years of operation, and ensure you have accurately addressed and gathered information on each of them.

Many creative sector entrepreneurs are overwhelmed with passion and don't address vital research as they should. That exciting phone call, the once in a lifetime meeting, and the opportunity out of the blue – when setting up a new business these are the things that distract entrepreneurs and prevent them from addressing the nuts and bolts research. You need to ascertain:

1. If your business is viable.

2. How to go about starting in a methodical way.

Having been involved with many start ups I have often seen the founders distracted by their excitement. When this happens, and as exciting as the trajectory may be, things inevitably fall through the cracks caused by lack of attention.

If there is one thing investors dislike it is loose ends. This happens when a revved up entrepreneur (which investors actually like) fails to dot the *i*s and cross the *t*s (which is something investors hate).

Of course in time you can employ people to address research and planning issues, but in the early days it is just you and it must be done carefully. Here is a checklist of some key areas that need to be researched before commencing a start up in the creative sector.

Market research

Before launching a business and spending money, you need to work out what your *point of difference* is.

It's one thing to be driven in the direction of your creative passion, but if you want to make it a commercial business you will need to ensure there is a genuine need for your product or service. This means researching target customers, competitors, market size and market trends.

Most commercial polling companies take polls of 200 to 1000 people. Therefore, if you poll 100 friends or even ask 100 people at the tube station or library (as long as you don't annoy them), you are likely to get a good cross sectional response to your product or idea. You could also try to get responses on Facebook or Twitter.

Research doesn't have to cost money, but it is imperative in determining if your idea is viable and to shape it to the market. You cannot market something well if the market doesn't want or need your product, or if you don't listen to what people do want to see in your product.

Business name

Researching your business name is very important. You need to choose a name that reflects your vision but also one that is not being used elsewhere. You can check this information via Companies House (**www.companieshouse.gov.uk**).

You can also visit the British Library Business & IP Centre (**www.bl.uk/bipc**) or one of its UK affiliates for a free check on trademark ownership. Using a lawyer to carry this out would cost a lot of money, but it is something you can do for yourself.

You can check domain name ownership on most domain name purchasing sites, or by visiting Whois (**www.whois.com**).

Finally, if your business is planning on utilising social media, you will need to make sure your desired *Twitter handle* is available and that you can choose a suitable Facebook name.

The law governing names usage relates to ownership of intellectual property (IP). As such, if your name is McDonald and you wanted to set up a hamburger shop using the name *McDonald's Burgers* you may well find a domain name that you like and is suitable. However, given that *McDonald's* owns global trademarks for that name for burger sales, their trademark will trump your domain name and they will most likely litigate against you.

Therefore researching the IP status of your name is the first step (after a good brainstorming session to select an ideal name) so that you avoid problems later. After this, simply lock in your names on the relevant forums. Then you are finished with name research.

Financial plan

Finances are covered in detail in a separate chapter, however financial research is critical before launching your start up. Whilst many creative ideas can be readily and significantly commercialised, it is imperative to do (at the very least) a *back of the envelope* financial scan to test viability. This is known as *financial research*.

You owe this to yourself as well as to any family and friends who may be providing cash to support you in your launch. Expensive accountants and software are not necessary.

You need to research the following financials:

- start-up costs
- break-even point
- sales targets
- balance sheet
- income statement
- cash flow statement

The primary data that goes into these figures should be easy for you to obtain. It is:

Start-up costs

You need to make calls, do Google searches and make whatever field trips are necessary to determine what money you will need. It is dangerous to underestimate these costs or to engage in wishful thinking about them. Proper research to get actual costs is imperative.

Expenses

Similarly to start-up costs, an accurate analysis of the costs you will incur in your first year of operation is very important. This should also be accurate and can be determined using real costs and a solid contingency of 10% to 20% (things always cost more than you budget).

Sales targets

Perhaps the hardest item to research is your sales potential. Most business plans and pitches overstate sales potential, but it is difficult to predict this accurately. It is, however, possible to research it through analysing competitor performance.

If there are any big public companies in your sector, research their publicly available information to get a feel for how they view your sector, the kind of comments they have made about it and the relevant benchmark financials they utilise. It is also perfectly reasonable to sit outside a competitor's store having a coffee witnessing the foot traffic going in and bags coming out.

Finally, you can obtain GDP data (which you can access online or at the British Library Business & IP Centre). GDP data will tell you the market size and GDP input or output of your sector. For example, you can view information on the creative sector and its impact on the UK economy on the UKTI website (**www.ukti.gov.uk**).

This can help you to ascertain the size of the pond you are swimming in and it gives you more information to complete your gut feel about possible revenue.

Strategic research

Researching the market is important to enable you to write your vision and mission for the business. It is also important to gather as much qualitative data as possible about your sector and the businesses in it to enable you to work out possible growth targets.

I attend hundreds of pitches each year and one of the things that always strikes me, as an investor and mentor, is when businesses know where they are going, or where they can go, in a broad sense.

Isn't it best to model yourself (and by that I do not mean copy but take inspiration from) on someone who has walked the path you want to walk? If you want to set up a fashion store, research the story of Sir Philip Green and Topshop. If you want to set up a florist, research the background of Interflora. Similarly, if creative digital media is your area, Spotify, Amazon and even challenged operations such as Napster would warrant research.

A final piece of research on the strategic front is entrepreneurs who have successfully exited businesses in your sector. This is like looking at websites of estate agents to see sales in your area when you are trying to sell your house. However, it's like doing it before you even buy your current house, so you know what you might sell it for in future years. If you buy a house for £200,000 and sales in your area are usually around £100,000, not only have you overpaid but your exit is going to be a very unhappy one where you lose money.

So research using tools such as Google, the *Economist* and all relevant trade publications for your niche. Most big exits, even those of private companies, are reported somewhere. This will give you something to aspire to. It will underwrite your confidence with realism and will reassure your investors that you are on a path to success.

Quick research tools

PEST

A helpful research tool you can use is the *PEST* analysis.

PEST stands for **P**olitical, **E**conomic, **S**ocial and **T**echnological Analysis and describes a framework of macro-environmental factors used in the environmental scanning component of strategic management.

- **Political factors** are basically to what degree the government intervenes in the economy. Specifically, areas such as tax policy, labour law, environmental law, trade restrictions, tariffs and political stability.

- **Economic factors** include economic growth, interest rates, exchange rates and the inflation rate. These factors have a major impact on how businesses operate and make decisions.

- **Social factors** include the cultural aspects and include health consciousness, population growth rate, age distribution, career attitudes and emphasis on safety. Trends in social factors affect the demand for a company's products and how that company operates.

- **Technological factors** include aspects such as research and development (R&D) activity, automation, technology incentives and the rate of technological change.

- **Environmental factors** include ecological and environmental aspects such as weather, climate and climate change, which may especially affect industries such as tourism, farming and insurance.

- **Legal factors** include discrimination law, consumer law, antitrust law, employment law and health and safety.

SWOT

Another tool some people find useful is SWOT. It stands for **S**trengths, **W**eaknesses, **O**pportunities and **T**hreats.

- **Strengths**: List all of the strengths of your business and concept.

- **Weaknesses**: List any weaknesses or vulnerabilities to your model for the business. These could be macro or micro; a poor economy or competition in your sector are examples.

- **Opportunities**: This means any opportunities your business can take advantage of to assist its growth. For example, in the creative sector an opportunity could be the government's and EU's recent policy focus on the creative and media industries.

- **Threats**: This is anything which literally threatens your business and its livelihood. It could be changing technology that would render your business obsolete or a competitor who has opened up and is entering into a price war with you.

CHOOSING A BUSINESS STRUCTURE

Different business structures are suited to different types of business. Many musicians, for example, are sole traders; many lawyers are in partnerships; and most operational companies that receive revenue from the public (e.g. retailers or online stores) are private limited companies.

I will run though the various types of business structure.

Sole trader

Sole tradership is the simplest business structure to operate. It refers to a real person who owns the business and is personally responsible for its debts. The owner of a sole proprietorship typically signs contracts in his or her own name.

Many businesses begin as sole traders and grow into more complex structures as the business develops.

This is a very risky structure and unnecessarily so. Many freelancers in the creative sector operate this way but as it creates maximum legal liability on the person it is not suitable in my view.

Partnership

A partnership is created when two or more persons engage in a business. Sometimes this is sealed with a handshake, but usually a formal agreement will be put in place.

Partnerships are commonly used in the area of professional services, like law firms, accounting firms and advisory firms, but not usually in the creative sector.

Social enterprise

Social enterprises are businesses set up to address a social or environmental need. Rather than maximising profit for shareholders or owners, profits are reinvested into the community or back into the business.

There are many social enterprises in the creative sector, including high profile ones like Doug Richard's School for Startups and the School for Creative Startups.

Private limited company

A private limited company is a traditional private company, separate from the owners, with its own rights and obligations. This is the commonest form of entity.

There are four main types of company:

1. **Private company limited by shares** – members' liability is limited to the amount they originally invested.

2. **Private company limited by guarantee** – members' liability is limited to the amount they have agreed to contribute to the company's assets if it is wound up.

3. **Private unlimited company** – there is no limit to the members' liability.

4. **Public limited company (PLC)** – the company's shares may be offered for sale to the general public and members' liability is limited to the amount they originally invested.

The vast majority of companies incorporated in the UK are private companies limited by shares, that is private limited liability companies.

As a general rule of thumb, incorporation is the most advantageous way of setting up a business. It protects the owner from personal liability, allows you to offset and carry losses, and it also means the business has its own legal recognition greater than you. This makes fundraising easier and is more attractive to partners and stakeholders. It just looks better as well as functioning in an optimal way.

*

Companies House (**www.companieshouse.gov.uk**) can provide more information on all these structures.

BUSINESS SYSTEMS

A business system is a structure that encapsulates your business idea. It is not a business model, but the methodology you use to operate your business.

When starting up, the type of business system you use is imperative, but it is often the last thing entrepreneurs think about. Those canny entrepreneurs who think long term will realise and enjoy the benefit of a utilising a business system that is right for them.

Choosing the right business system can:

- Make business easier

- Ensure you achieve exponential growth

- Expedite your path to success

- Create a sum of parts that is greater than the whole, so the business can outlive the founder

- Enable your business to expand, scale and, if you wish, globalise – faster

- Deliver greater efficiency to your business

Business is not always easy, but just as you can make running easier by being fit in the first place, you can make business easier by having the right business physique.

I will discuss the following four types of business systems and look at some examples of businesses that use them:

1. Franchise

2. Licence agreement

3. Joint venture

4. Merger

1. Franchise

Franchising is an excellent business system if you are creating a brand which you feel will have strong *brand equity* in the eyes of the public. Famous franchises in Britain include McDonald's, Costa, Subway, 7-Eleven, Europcar and Hilton Hotels.

How a franchise works

A franchise is established in this series of steps:

1. An entrepreneur buys or sets up a business which is marketable to the public (i.e. a business to consumer, or B to C, business).

2. A bible of systems, tools and procedures as to how the business is going to be built and operated is put in place. This is basically a formula for how the business is run.

3. The brand is built carefully, with attention paid to everything the brand stands for and ensuring as much *brand equity* as possible is developed.

4. The business is launched in a pilot market.

5. Once it is established and successful, after say two years, mini varieties of the business are sold to others in the business' home country and/or master franchise rights are sold abroad (i.e. rights are sold to operate that business in other countries).

6. In the case of home-country sales, an upfront fee and a royalty of gross sales will be charged by franchiser to franchisee. With overseas sales, a larger fee will usually be charged and a smaller royalty.

If you are thinking of buying a franchise or want advice on how to set your business up from the start so it can be franchisable, Franchise Development Services (**www.fdsfranchise.com**) are the UK's leading consultants.

Many creative sector businesses operate as franchises, offering a simple entry point for creative sector entrepreneurs (if they have capital available). Many franchisers offer their own financing programmes also, which means if you are not able to borrow from a bank you may still be able to buy one. Franchises are for sale across a wide range of creative sector industries including entertainment, beauty, floristry, photography and advertising.

I will cover more about franchises in the section 'Buying a Business'.

Focus on creative sector franchises

There have been some hugely successful franchises in the creative sector. Let's take a look at how a couple of them built their businesses using this system.

MANGO

The MANGO fashion chain offers its franchise system throughout the EU and in other major world cities. The MANGO franchise places at your disposal a comprehensive system that covers all aspects relating to product marketing and franchise management. As a global fashion powerhouse, MANGO has become a household name as a brand, synonymous with quality clothing at reasonable prices.

It is relatively common for major fashion businesses to operate as franchises, since fashion is often market specific and needs local knowledge from a hands-on partner.

MANGO, as franchisor, provides the clothing, accessories, store design, training, merchandising and ongoing sales assistance. This is done through ongoing dialogue and periodic site visits. As franchisee, you do the rest.

Remember that it is going to be easier to gain finance and get a good location in a storel with a MANGO franchise then with a store no one has heard of. That's the advantage of franchising – you can exploit MANGO's brand for your benefit.

www.mango.com

Gloria Jean's Coffees

I have been involved with large-scale franchises, including Australian-owned global coffee chain Gloria Jean's Coffee, on whose board I sat for some years. Gloria Jean's has stores in over 42 countries and, apart from two, all are franchises, meaning they have sold the rights for that country to a local partner.

This is only possible because Gloria Jean's has a solid reputation (brand) and was successful in its home market of Australia, where it was regularly voted Franchiser of the Year. This assisted greatly in its global growth. As such, Gloria Jean's considers itself to be in the franchising business as well as the coffee business.

Gloria Jean's vision is: *To be the most loved and respected coffee company worldwide.*

Gloria Jean's expands in three ways:

1. Some markets are owned by the parent company.

2. Some markets are sold completely (under master franchise arrangements) where the rights for a whole country are sold to a franchisee.

3. Within the markets it owns, Gloria Jean's sells individual franchises. For example, in Australia there are over 400 franchisee stores.

Gloria Jean's has made a big success out of good coffee and also having franchise know-how. This allows it to expand in a cost-effective manner.

As with any good franchise, the vision, mission, values and brand reputation are of key importance. It is important that all franchisees buy into the vision and work collectively to achieve it. This further enhances *brand equity* for each country and the parent company.

While I looked after Gloria Jean's in Europe, we were working to sell rights to many nations and there are currently stores in Ireland, Kazakhstan, Turkey, Ukraine and Cyprus, to name just a few.

The master franchise arrangement

When setting up a master franchise, Gloria Jean's looks for the following in a candidate:

- Partnership based on integrity and trust
- Commitment to excellence and innovation
- A culture of joy and passion
- Belief in people, and building and changing lives
- A **M**aster **F**ranchise **P**artner (MFP) candidate must embrace the vision, mission and values of Gloria Jean's.

Additionally, the MFP candidate must have a clear understanding of the mutual goals and commitments necessary for the success of the multi-unit retail service business and must be willing to commit the necessary human and financial resources to successfully develop, manage and promote their Gloria Jean's branches.

Financed, highly visible companies with plans to diversify may be suitable MFP candidates, provided that they are willing to make the necessary commitment to employ and retain the services of a qualified and capable management team with related experience and expertise.

An MFP candidate should have sufficient capital to adequately finance the business, including the necessary banking relationships to obtain the financing required to develop the minimum number of outlets throughout the ten-year development term.

www.gloriajeanscoffees.com

2. Licence agreement

Where a franchise is often used for the expansion of a consumer brand, IP (intellectual property) owners often use a licence agreement.

A licensor may grant a licence under intellectual property laws to authorise a use (such as copying software or using a patented invention) to a licensee, sparing the licensee from a claim of infringement brought by the licensor. A licence agreement generally has term, territory and renewal provisions as key elements.

In the creative sector, licensing would typically be used by anyone who owns intellectual property that is of value and other people want to use. Examples include software owners (e.g. digital media and game IP owners). Another common usage is those who own performance rights, for example music publishers, songwriters, musicians and producers (for TV, theatre, film, etc.).

Licence agreements provide strict guidelines as to how the format and IP can be used at the same time as allowing for the owner of the IP to access markets around the world through local partners who have the infrastructure, capital and know-how to take the intangible IP and turn it into a viable business.

The licencing business model with usually involves an upfront fee and a royalty.

With *Dirty Dancing* we used licensing to expand around the world. The first deal we did was to licence European rights, for which we received a substantial sum upfront and an ongoing royalty. The day-to-day show operations were undertaken by leading European entertainment company Stage Entertainment. We provided the brand and IP (that is the name *Dirty Dancing* for theatrical usage) and the show know-how.

3. Joint venture

A joint venture is an excellent way to operate if there is more than one party – usually two – with distinct but complementary skill sets that are both necessary to bring a vision to life.

Like an engagement is to a marriage, a joint venture becomes a quasi-legal entity in its own right whilst each party maintains its own identity. That is to say the companies do not merge, one does not acquire the other and one is not more passive than the other overall. It would usually be governed by a joint venture agreement specifying what each party is to bring to the table and what aspects of the business each party will fulfil.

A joint venture typically has a specific purpose and is not intended to operate ad infinitum. All profits, losses and distributions would be shared equally – usually 50/50 or *pari pasu*, depending on the number of parties to the venture.

It is an excellent way for a start up to gain traction quickly because if it can collaborate with another business, which itself may also be a start up, no money needs to change hands, however a broader entity can be created.

Additionally, a joint venture can allow a creative sector entrepreneur to partner with a business person who may have expertise, for example, in distribution or some other business area. As such, the creative entrepreneur can focus on creating the product or service whilst the partner can focus on the business side.

Focus on Live Nation Entertainment

Live Nation, the world's largest entertainment conglomerate, often makes use of joint ventures, especially when expanding into markets in which it wishes to draw upon a particular expertise, or where it may not have the extensive experience it has in other markets.

Here is a media release announcing one of their significant joint ventures. It shows the mechanics of two major companies coming together with different strengths to follow a common purpose. It shows how with joint ventures, the underlying concept is that the sum of the parts is greater then the whole.

Live Nation Entertainment, Inc. and *Creativeman Productions* in Tokyo, Japan, recently announced the formation of *Live Nation Japan*, a joint venture between the two companies.

> **❝** *We are very pleased to announce Live Nation's entry into Japan and to have such a credible partner as Creativeman, which has a long and proven track record of promoting major artists as well as developing highly successful festivals,"* said Michael Rapino, President and Chief Executive Officer of Live Nation Entertainment. *"Expanding our presence in Asia reflects our commitment to growing our business internationally in a region that is becoming increasingly important for touring artists.* **❞**

> **❝** *We are very excited to be a part of Live Nation Japan and for Creativeman this is an important milestone that opens up many exciting opportunities,"* said Naoki Shimizu, CEO of Creativeman. *"Creativeman and Live Nation Japan will together be able to bring more concerts to Japan, develop existing and new festivals and also leverage Live Nation's vast experience of promoting some of the best tours globally.* **❞**

Creativeman is the leading promoter of international artists in Japan, the second largest live music market in the world. They are also the producers of the iconic Summer Sonic festival, which reached record breaking attendance in 2011, with 200,000 attendees in Tokyo and Osaka.

The first concert for Live Nation Japan will be Lady Gaga's *Born This Way Ball* in Tokyo.

4. Merger

A merger is a marriage where the joint venture was an engagement. It is effectively defined as two companies becoming one. Usually a merger is reserved for more mature companies and it is typically employed where a company wishes to expand, or integrate vertically or horizontally.

Horizontal integration is a merger with another company in the same industry, for example one method Live Nation has employed to expand is to buy out other promoters in selected global markets.

The media release on the occasion of the merger of Live Nation and Ticketmaster (shown below) represents *vertical integration*. This is when two companies in the same supply chain unite through a common owner to crystallise cost or efficiency savings or create added value.

Focus on Live Nation

A notable creative sector merger also involved Live Nation – in 2010 it merged with ticketing provider Ticketmaster in a $4.4bn deal. This shows a large-scale example of vertical integration, where the creative content provider (Live Nation) merged with the distribution channel (Ticketmaster).

The release shows you how complex such a business deal can be due to the effects that a merger can have on the market, its choice and what it pays for the products post-merger. This merger in particular was a political *hot potato*.

Here is that media release:

> A merger between *Ticketmaster* and concert promoter *Live Nation* has been cleared by the UK's Competition Commission following a challenge by a rival ticket agency which concluded the deal would not lead to a "substantial lessening" of competition in UK ticket retailing. The US Justice Department had previously allowed the merger.

Ticketmaster Entertainment and the world's largest concert promoter, Live Nation, completed their merger after agreeing with U.S. antitrust officials to divest some assets. The new *Live Nation Entertainment* will own more than 140 concert venues globally, sell around 140 million tickets a year and promote 22,000 concerts annually.

BUYING A BUSINESS

Buying a business is often the best route to get into business for start up creative entrepreneurs.

I have used it many times as a means to break into a new area. I have bought and sold several businesses in the past 15 years and experience tells me that mistakes and *good luck* both come from the way in which the buying process starts and operates. Fatal mistakes are made at the beginning of a deal.

As a start up creative entrepreneur, you may be trying to get your passion off the ground at the same time as holding down a job, studying or raising kids. When time is in short supply like this, buying a business can shortcut many years of work (although it does bring its own pitfalls).

If you find a good business, research it well and have a clear idea of what it is worth to you. You need a concise timeline to buy and take control of it; if you do this it will auger well for the future.

Like buying a house, if you become emotionally involved in the purchase, pay above the odds or allow the buying process to be a long, strung-out courtship with no consummation, the chances are that you will lose focus and start to gloss over possible problems in the desperation to seal the deal.

When I have bought medium to large businesses, I brought a commercial advisor into my corner as a steady hand. When buying a start up business this is not in the budget, however it is always a good idea to bring a family member or friend into the mix before you begin so that they can provide a wise head to keep you calm, rational and focused.

Focus on the Capitol Theatre, Sydney

In Australia I was the chairman of the Capitol Theatre, a beautiful 2000 seat lyric theatre and one of the leading theatres in Australasia. Many amazing shows played there, including *Miss Saigon*, *The Lion King*, *Billy Elliot* and *Wicked*.

The time came when the independent directors of the board decided it was the right market to sell the theatre. A tender process was launched through a major investment bank, which cost a fortune and failed to produce any serious buyers, just competitors who wanted to look at our company books and records.

Later, over a casual coffee, a little known but successful entrepreneur expressed an interest in buying the theatre. A valuation had already been done and we knew the price he was offering was more than fair. Already in the entertainment sector, the buyer had clearly identified that he wanted the theatre and he knew his business.

The prospective buyer had undertaken substantial research and was aware of the historical bookings at the theatre. He was aware of potential future bookings through discussions within his current network, media articles and entertainment websites. After talks we put pen to paper and chiselled out a timeline which was aggressive yet generous enough to ensure every step of the legal process was covered properly.

As entrepreneurs we had agreed the key points, but needed to bring in lawyers to undertake legal and financial due diligence, i.e. for the buyer to ensure everything presented to him was accurate. Once this stage was over, the buyer advised us his funding source was secure.

Legal and financial due diligence is imperative prior to any funds being made available to a buyer by their lender, and even if the buyer is paying cash and not borrowing the funds.

Finally, the day came to complete the sale. The buyer visited our office and together with our lawyers we did a *page turn*. This is the legal term for the buyer, seller and their lawyers sitting in a room with bottomless cups of coffee going through each and every page in the sale agreement to ensure everyone is happy, that no pages have been changed from those agreed, and it is acceptable for both parties to sign. After this process, which took some hours, the documents were signed with much fanfare.

The buyer has made the theatre even more successful than before. He has since bought the other major theatre in Sydney and has been able to capitalise on the economies of scale by owning both venues, sharing costs and operating the business efficiently.

The buyer was not a start up entrepreneur, but the clear and concise strategic plan he had in mind and executed allowed him to become extremely successful in the venue ownership sector, a sector he had minimal presence in before he bought out the theatre.

So let's look at the buying process from a start up perspective.

Buying process from a start up perspective

Finding

Firstly you need to have an idea in your mind of the sector in which you want to buy. It should be related to the sector you are passionate about or in which you have experience or knowledge.

Then finding a business to buy is as simple as visiting a business broker website or reading the relevant creative sector trade publications.

These publications are a good way to get a feel for your part of the creative sector and the players in it before you proceed to enquire about the particular business that is of interest to you.

If you do find a business, be sure to always consider the sector, size, turnover, location and who is selling the business. There are a few ways to determine whether it's the right one for you:

1. Think about whether the buyer is in a hurry to sell. If so find out why. There may be hidden problems such as debt or a large fall in profits.

2. Check the finances. Look at turnover, profits and accounts.

3. Have a look at the customer base.

4. The status of the employees is important – is there a strong team?

5. You should also analyse the competitors.

Obviously, the most important thing to look at when deciding whether a business is the right one for you is what you're likely to pay for it. Research is imperative to confirm whether you can actually afford it and if the business is worth the asking price.

To find a business, start with the British Business Brokers Association (**ukbusinessesforsale.com**). This is a non-profit body that operates solely in the best interests of people and firms engaged in the various aspects of business transfers in the UK.

Funding

Funding the acquisition of a start up usually requires help from family and friends, unless you have some hard asset such as a house that you can borrow against. It is also possible to use your own funds.

The banks in Britain are unfortunately not in favour of lending to start up entrepreneurs to buy a business, unless you are buying a franchise, in which case the funding options are different. Banks lend up to 75% of the purchase price of a franchise. They do this because they feel safe that the franchise is a solid brand with proven systems, tools and procedures commensurate with successful performance. In the area of franchising, several major banks including HSBC, NatWest and Lloyds, lend for purchases.

If the bank decides to lend you the money that could well be the green light to go ahead. Before you get to that stage though, there are certain things the bank will want to know.

They will want to see a cash flow forecast for your first year of trading. You also need to have prepared a budget plan, business plan and, as I mentioned earlier, a solid income or hard asset to borrow against.

If you don't have sufficient funds personally and are unable to get funding from a bank, family and friends are your best option. Indeed, family and friends is the way most start up entrepreneurs in the creative sector gain funding, especially in order to buy a business. This is not the easy option; in fact borrowing from family and friends can present many complications and they may hold you to account more strongly than any normal investor would. If you borrow from family and friends, however, it can be the leg-up you need to make the purchase.

Buying into a franchise

Franchising is an excellent way for creative sector entrepreneurs to buy into a business because they are buying a *business in a box* with established systems, tools and procedures, and with a solid, known brand.

The steps would be:

1. Contact Franchise Development Services (**www.fdsfranchise.com**) or search Google for *business brokers*. You may also buy the *Franchise Magazine* (**www.thefranchisemagazine.net**) or contact the British Franchise Association (**www.thebfa.org**). You can also attend the British Franchising Exhibition trade show or one of a number of trade shows run throughout the year where there are many stalls with franchises on offer and associated support services.

2. Find a franchise in the creative sector you like. There are plenty of them.

3. Ascertain the cost and do your own research, as suggested in the research chapter.

4. Speak to a bank's franchise department about their lending policies.

5. Make the acquisition.

Buying a franchise is simple. It reduces a lot of the time and effort that needs to be spent buying a business and it can enable you to start up with an established brand that has a proven modus operandi.

Valuation

Valuation is one of the most important things to get right in the process of buying a business. Unfortunately, it's also one of the most difficult. You need to know that you're paying the right price for the business you've set your heart on. The only way of doing this is to carry out in-depth research.

The minimum information you will need to look at when buying is:

- Balance sheet
- Income statement
- Cash flow projections
- Bank statements
- Important contracts (i.e. with suppliers, leases, utilities, etc.)
- Tax returns

To assess the overall viability of the business, speak with customers and suppliers as well as the vendor. That may give you information about the business, or even the market in general, that you might not have considered checking.

You should also find out why it's being sold. If the previous owner has to sell it because of a fall in profits, for example, it will bring the price of the business down.

Deciding upon a price

Anyone can buy something if they are prepared to pay enough. Obviously as a buyer your job is to get the asset for the best price you can. Similarly the seller wants to get the best price they can.

Working out a price you can both agree on is based on:

- Your valuation
- The seller's valuation
- Negotiation, as the fugures will rarely be the same

Businesses are valued based on the *price-to-earnings ratio* (how many times the earnings of the business you are prepared to pay). For example, if a business has an earnings before interest and tax of £20,000 and the industry standard price-to-earnings ratio (P/E) is 4, you may consider £80,000 to be a fair price.

However, the seller will usually try and push for a higher P/E valuation (based on their projections for the future) and will also include *goodwill*. Goodwill is an intangible asset which is basically the company's brand, their customer base and the intangible reputation the seller has built up for the business.

You may also be buying hard assets as part of the purchase, including stock,and perhaps the lease if the store has a retail outlet and hard goods such as technological equipment. Stock would normally be bought at cost if it is less than a year old. Hard goods would normally be bought at their book value.

Once you have looked at all these factors, you should be able to work out a *return on investment* (ROI). A business is really only worth anything if it can pay for itself over a reasonable period of time. You want to make a profit as soon as you can.

The business plan

The next stage in setting out your groundwork is drafting your business plan. In the case of an acquisition, a 120-day plan would *not* be the only tool you need.

If you are obtaining funding you may need a full business plan. Even if you are not, you will need a plan in place so you know what you are going to do with the business strategically and how you will add value to the business once you have bought it. If the plan does not show you adding value to the business you should not be buying it.

A person always has reasons for selling their business and they are rarely sinister. Sometimes a business has had a *season* with a particular owner and they have reached their capacity or lost their passion for it. The buyer needs to be full of passion and use their untapped capacity to add value where the seller can no longer do so or does not wish to.

Timetable for acquisition

It is imperative to set a timetable for buying the business. The timing is not always in your control as a buyer, but it is important to sit with the seller and once you have agreed the key terms, to set a timetable you both agree on and feel is reasonable.

The process need not be long and drawn out and, once you have funding in place, it can be completed in four weeks. The area where things can slow down is during the financial and legal due diligence, but this should not take more than two to three weeks if you know what you are doing or if you have a good accountant, lawyer or advisor on board.

Lawyers will also need to draw up a contract for sale, although you can obtain templates online. Even if you do obtain one online, it is still advisable to have a lawyer look over it to ensure it covers everything and is governed by the relative jurisdiction. There is no point having a wonderful contract drawn up under USA law for a UK deal.

I have learned that as much as start up entrepreneurs hope to save money, there is a time and place where money needs to be spent. Obtaining good advice from lawyers can enhance the value of the business you are buying, save you wasting money on mistakes and will be something you will be grateful for in the long run.

This does not mean you need to spend a small fortune on lawyers and get what I call *fee fatigue*, but it means you should set aside a reasonable amount of money to ensure you can have good people looking at your documentation.

*

You can get more free information on buying a business from Small Business UK (**www.smallbusiness.co.uk**).

STARTING A CREATIVE SECTOR BUSINESS AT HOME

It is possible to start a creative sector business from scratch at home. If you want to do this, here are some suggestions of platforms you can use to sell your goods.

notonthehighstreet.com

Not On The High Street is perfect for arts and crafts makers who need a platform to sell from.

How notonthehighstreet.com works

The site brings together over 3,000 independent, small UK businesses that between them sell over 60,000 products through a single checkout. It provides a route to market for thousands of designer-makers and creative businesses, who might otherwise struggle for custom and can lose out in the wholesale battle with high street giants. Businesses are selected for the site if they are innovative, with well-made products to inspire shoppers looking for style, originality and quality, but who never seem to find it on the high street.

notonthehighstreet.com say:

> **“** We're passionate about working with talented, creative people with exceptionally high standards; people who are committed to their roles, their careers and to the company. We work hard on developing talent with training, mentoring, and internal promotion, and we value people who seek responsibility and ownership. We aim to provide a fun place to work, with regular social activities and a focus on working together. Above all we're dedicated to supporting small businesses and delivering a first-class experience to all our customers. **”**

www.notonthehighstreet.com

Jamie At Home

Jamie at Home is Jamie Oliver's party plan business which was launched in March 2009. With no prior experience needed, it is open to everyone.

Jamie at Home says:

> **"** Are you looking for a job which fits around your family life or just something to supplement your monthly income? If your answer is yes, Jamie at Home could be the answer!

"Jamie's is sold around the country by a 3,800 strong team of men and women. Jamie at Home consultants earn a minimum of 20% commission on all products sold at their parties. Direct selling consultants also achieve additional bonuses and incentives. You can work flexible hours, have a full-time career or earn some extra cash on the side. **"**

www.jamieathome.com

The Pampered Chef

The Pampered Chef is run through a network of independent consultants who earn income and have time freedom.

The Pampered Chef says they are:

> **"** The premier direct seller of essential kitchen tools, and has been helping families prepare quick, delicious meals since 1999. **"**

Dedicated to fostering entrepreneurship, The Pampered Chef has a reputation for providing solutions to those who want a start up business which can be run around life commitments and out of hours.

www.pamperedchef.co.uk

ETSY

The Etsy online global marketplace is a great way to grow an independent creative sector business. Etsy is a vibrant community of 15 million buyers and creative businesses. You can grow your brand with a wealth of new customers and promotional tools.

Etsy say:

> **❝**There are no membership fees with Etsy.
> It costs $0.20 to list an item for 4 months or until it sells.
> Once you sell your item we collect a 3.5% fee on the sale price.
> Share the story of your craft in your profile, item photos, and shop banner.
> Escape the 9-5 grind and focus on your passion. **❞**

www.etsy.com

Forming Bands

Forming Bands is a group of musicians, based in Bristol and London, who've played in bands together and apart for the last 15 years, and who have developed a business around getting bands together.

If you are musically inclined and trying to make a business as a freelance musician, it can help you be noticed, get gigs and also find partners to collaborate with.

www.formingbands.co.uk

Base79

FOR ASHLEY MACKENZIE, son of broadcaster and former *Sun* editor Kelvin, a career in media seemed inevitable. His company, Base79, is a business-to-business firm that helps owners of original video content distribute, protect and monetise their material online.

Base79 works with the creators of all kinds of entertainment – from music videos to sports highlight packages – before distributing the content to YouTube, Hulu and Dailymotion, to name just some.

Building on his seed funding, MacKenzie completed a Series A funding round worth £2.75m, which enabled him to pursue international expansion.

MacKenzie says:

❝ In our business, we work with content partners, and the US represents the biggest international acquirer of content and the biggest exporter of content. We felt it was important to get a presence here, a statement of intent more than anything.

"The UK TV ad market is worth $6bn dollars a year; the US TV ad market is worth about $72bn dollars a year… this is a huge market, which is showing no signs of slowing down. As our business has evolved, a lot of bets that we've made, such as the rise of YouTube and social media, have come true, and we think we're well-positioned to understand the changing content world. ❞

www.base79.com

Granger and Co

AUSTRALIAN CELEBRITY CHEF BILL GRANGER has hugely successful cafes and restaurants in Australia and Japan. He moved into the British market first through his media presence of TV shows and recipe books. Bill then opened a store in Notting Hill which has become a massive success – with long lines of patrons often snaking around the corner. It's great Australian food!

So Bill is now a multimedia creative sector entrepreneur and is a contributor to *Waitrose* magazine. With television shows presented on the Lifestyle channel regularly, he has combined a media presence with a successful core business.

It is all centred around his passion for food and taking this vision to the world.

www.grangerandco.com

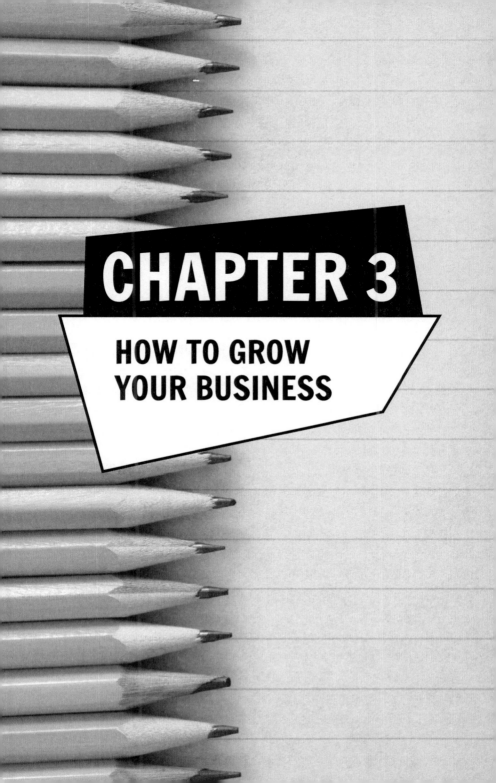

CHAPTER 3

HOW TO GROW
YOUR BUSINESS

THE BIGGEST MISTAKES WHEN STARTING A BUSINESS

When considering how to grow a business I want to start by looking at the mistakes you can make that will hold your business back and prevent it from growing.

Mistakes do happen and if you get a result that is not what was desired, or not what is good for your stakeholders, employees or the business as a whole, usually a new strategy can be employed to turn things around. However, it is best to model other successful businesses and research mistakes others have made in order to avoid making them yourself.

I have studied the mistakes and failures of many business leaders and entrepreneurs and here are the top ten:

1. Undercapitalisation
2. Believing others will automatically fall in love with the business
3. Bad advice
4. Trying the same strategy and expecting a different result
5. Business with partners
6. Thinking you are bigger than the market
7. Growth that is too rapid
8. Being controlling
9. Not paying on time
10. Having a selective focus

I will discuss these in turn now.

1. Undercapitalisation

You will always need more money than you think. Do not sugarcoat your budget or try to make the costs lower in order to make the numbers work. Some of my angel investments have done this and I have learned that just as with our own personal finances, things always cost more.

This is where research is vital. Do your research, have your costs in actual terms and then ensure you have a 20% contingency.

These strategies will not only keep you from blowing your head off with stress when things do cost more, but will also appease investors and banks too as it will make them more comfortable that the numbers are real. You will gain respect from them as you won't appear naïve.

2. Believing others will automatically fall in love with the business

Many creative sector entrepreneurs believe that because their business is so exciting, their products so lovely and their services so unique, they are a dead certainty for global adoration. This is not the case; there will always be a percentage of people who will love what you do and a percentage that won't.

I have promoted major concert artists in the past who were top of the charts and yet lost money on the tour. Conversely, we have promoted lesser known artists who sold out venues unexpectedly. For example, about ten years ago we signed up a little known artist called Usher to tour Australia. By the time the tour came around he was number one and the tour sold out. Life works like this sometimes.

What we need to learn from these situations is that investors and stakeholders will not forgive weakness in your business strategy or shortcomings in your plans just because you are a creative person.

They will tell you to leave the business world and do it as a hobby.

If you want to make a business from your creative passion you need to treat people with respect and realise they will not be overawed by just one side of the business offering. You need to show you know both sides.

3. Bad advice

Bad advice is a killer. I have lost legal cases with bad lawyers and the worst deal I ever did with bad advice lost me over £10m. It was such a simple deal I thought that I only needed a cheap lawyer. Well he screwed it up and I really paid for it.

Do not scrimp when paying for advice. Just as a doctor failing to spot a serious health issue will be dangerous in the long term, bad business advice can rob you of profits or even send you bankrupt.

You don't need to be shelling out thousands on top-tier law and accounting firms. You just need to find recommendations for those who specialise in small and growing creative sector businesses and seek their advice.

You need a mentor also, which can be a professional like me, or a family member or friend you trust and who knows about business. They may also be a good font of knowledge for recommendations.

4. Trying the same strategy and expecting a different result

This is the definition of insanity, yet many do it in business.

Be true to your vision and mission, but be flexible enough to change course mid-race. You need to constantly ask yourself how your creative product or service is being received by the market, and if something is not working change it and change it fast (after research and testing if possible).

Let your gut feel and your advisors guide you, but if something doesn't produce the results you want in a decent period, try something else. Be obsessive and try incessantly to master your mission and achieve your vision through whatever means are successful.

5. Business with partners

Having a partner can complement your own strengths and weaknesses and can provide a constant teammate and cheerleader, but be careful about taking on partners, especially ones with an emotional connection to you such as family and friends.

Creative businesses are often driven by emotion and centred on intangible assets, making them hard to split if there is a fall out, and heightening the emotion of the business.

One of my businesses was a series of companies with my family. It ended in litigation and recriminations all around. I have also had some negative experiences with business partners and friends who I believe took advantage of me.

It is always hard to make two people agree 100% of the time but, like a marriage, you may find someone that you gel with and with whom you want to do business. Ensure you have an agreement with your partners, that it is clear and put it in writing.

6. Thinking you are bigger than the market

The *market* is the market as a whole – the economy, the market you are selling to, the competitors, etc. No one is bigger than the market. Make sure you do not get too big for your boots, believing your way is the only way and if your customers don't like it they are wrong.

Neither should you get angry with your investors for criticising your methods and do not get disappointed when people you expect to embrace your ideas question them.

The market is there now and will be there in 100 years – it's your job to fit in and educate the market about your product, all the while having an inherent respect for it. If you go with the market, it's like riding a wave on a surfboard. If you go against it, you can get dumped on the sand by a big wave.

7. Growth that is too rapid

Growth needs to be measured. Whilst being the next Google or Facebook is a great aim, the reality is most companies take time to develop, like a baby crawling and then walking.

If you go from start up to massive growth too fast you will miss out on a formative time in the business which means the foundation will not be as solid as it could be. Also, growing too rapidly can burn cash (look at the dot-com businesses of the 1990s) and lead to silly errors.

Stick to your plan. You can hope for overnight success but even if you have one, make sure the foundation is laid carefully so that the growth is built on a solid footing.

8. Being controlling

You need to know how to delegate or you will not have an easy time. Many creative sector entrepreneurs – and entrepreneurs in general – are self-confessed control freaks. This can be a positive and can ensure you are on top of everything, however you need to harness this for its positive aspects and manage it well. You need to have systems, delegate, outsource and let people do their thing.

In many start up creative businesses there is little money to pay people – your employees (if you have them) will be there because they love you and the business. Communicate your vision and the company's mission and values to them, and let them get on with their job.

You need to work on the business and as a start up you may also need to work in it. Some days are for working *in* the business – doing ordinary, day-to-day business tasks – and some days are for working *on* it – that is strategising and visualising.

9. Not paying on time

Do not think that because you are a start up you do not have to pay people on time and they will forgive you. I have had people do this to me and I can tell you it is majorly disrespectful. Money is the currency of business. Unless someone agrees to waive their fee or to accept generous payment terms in advance, they need to be paid on time.

If you don't pay a bill you may receive a *letter of demand*. This will give you seven days to pay and, if not, the creditor may legally send a debt collector to collect the debt or issue with you a statutory demand. A *statutory demand* is very serious as if you don't pay up or have grounds to dispute it, you can be wound up in 21 days.

To avoid all of this just pay your bills. Communicate with your creditors if you can't and try to negotiate a payment plan in writing. If this not in writing it is not a legal plan and the debt is not legally deferred.

10. Having a selective focus

Focusing only on specific matters is a big mistake, especially in creative sector businesses. You need to focus on all the areas I talk about in this book and all the items your advisors tell you about.

I know tax, administration and financials may bore you, but introduce systems to deal with everything and ensure every aspect is covered. If there are items you really can't stand, get advice from your mentor about outsourcing that particular item, or advertise for someone to help you, e.g. a bookkeeper.

HOW TO WRITE A BUSINESS PLAN

In the growth phase of your business you are most likely looking to expand, scale up and raise further funds. Creative sector businesses often start off as single person operators and then reach the stage where they need to take on people, premises or invest in infrastructure in order to generate more business.

I have already discussed the 120-day plan, which is in essence a short and simple business plan. However, in order to scale effectively a proper business plan must be written. It is not necessary to employ expensive consultants to do this as it is relatively simple and I will cover the key areas you need to address.

As a guide, it might take four weeks to complete the plan, including research and tying things together. It is impossible to write a business plan without thorough research, and knowledge of your creative business and the industry as a whole. Research is where the time is spent; the actual writing is easy.

The business plan is designed to educate someone who knows little about your business and the elements of the creative sector in which you operate. As such, you need to make it simple, concise and over explain any nuances you may be familiar with but with which outsiders to your business are not.

Just about everyone I mentor asks me how to write a business plan. There are many templates and other information sources online, many books have been written on the subject, and accountants and lawyers can help. Yet it seems to be an area in which many people just don't know where to start or what is appropriate for their business.

Business plans need to be more than just a nice looking, detailed document to go in someone's bottom draw. They need to be living documents that serve their purpose – to educate stakeholders about your business and to successfully obtain funding.

I have listed below the critical line items I believe you need in the plan. You can use the resources I mention above to research them further.

Critical items in a business plan

Products and services

- What are they?

Competitive advantages

- Marketing plan
- Market research
- Product, price, place, promotion
- Branding information
- USP

Operational plan for legal matters (IP and other legal considerations)

- Production and inventory details
- Employees
- Suppliers

Management and organisation

Information regarding who the following are in your organisation:

- Management advisory board
- Lawyer
- Accountant

- Insurance agent

- Bank

- Consultant

- Mentors and key advisors

Macro-economic analysis

- Economic analysis

- Analysis of the broad economy

- Analysis of the specific sector you are entering and its economy

Competitive analysis

- Who are your competitors and how are their businesses faring?

- SWOT

Financials

Start up expenses and capitalisation

- Financial plan

- Key ratios

- Balance sheet (actual or projected)

- Income statement (actual or projected)

Fundraising

For bankers and lenders

- Bankers want assurance of orderly repayment. If you intend to present this plan to lenders, include:
    - Amount of funds being sought
    - How the funds will be used
    - How they will be applied – how it will make the business stronger
    - Requested repayment terms (number of years to repay)
    - Collateral or security offered

For angels

- Funds needed short term
- Funds needed in two to five years
- How the company will use the funds and what this will accomplish for growth
- Estimated return on investment
- Exit strategy for investors (buyback, sale, etc.)
- Percentage of ownership that you will give to investors
- Milestones or conditions that you will accept
- Financial reporting to be provided
- Involvement of investors on the board or in management

Appendices

- Brochures and advertising materials
- Industry studies
- Maps and photos of location

- Magazine or other articles
- Detailed lists of equipment owned or to be purchased
- Copies of leases and contracts
- Letters of support from customers
- Any other materials needed to support the assumptions in the plan
- Market research studies
- List of assets available as security for any loan

Other information to include

Many creative sector businesses sell intangible products. They are usually more flexible than other types of businesses, but they also have higher labour costs and generally few hard assets:

- What are the key competitive factors in this industry?
- Your prices
- Methods used to set prices
- System of production management
- Percentage of work subcontracted to other firms. Will you make a profit on sub-contracting?
- Credit, payment, and collections policies and procedures
- Strategy for keeping clients

Digital media companies

High-tech companies sometimes have to operate for a longer time without making a profit and sometimes even without sales. These should include:

- Economic outlook for the industry
- Will the company have information systems in place to monitor prices, costs and markets?

- Will they be on the cutting edge with your products and services?

- Information regarding research and development and what is required to:

  - Bring product/service to market

  - Keep the company competitive

- How does the company:

  - Protect IP

  - Avoid technological obsolescence

  - Supply necessary capital

  - Retain key people

PROOF OF CONCEPT

In order to grow your business and in many cases to gain funding, you will need to go through the *proof of concept* phase. This is exactly as it says – proving the concept and proving to the market (and yourself) that the business model works and refining it if necessary.

Proof of concept has many different names over the various segments of the creative sector, including *prototyping*, *beta testing* and *test screening*.

Here are some examples.

- In filmmaking Pixar sometimes creates short animated films that use an untested technique. Their short film *Geri's Game* used techniques for animation of cloth and of human facial expressions later employed in *Toy Story 2*. Similarly, Pixar created several short films as proofs of concept for new techniques to be used later in the production of *Finding Nemo*.

- Advertising agencies bring in test groups to review advertisements before they are released to television.

- Theatre producers undertake preview performances which are sold for cheaper than normal ticket prices and are used to test audience reactions and iron out technical, sound and lighting issues.

- Music producers will also undertake proof of concept by the record company releasing *single* from an album to test the public's reaction and gauge download and sales numbers.

- In digital media game and app production the designers have players test the games, looking for faults and ease/difficulty.

- A prototype is often used as part of the product design process and to validate the design. Another common strategy is to design, test, evaluate and then improve the design based on reaction to and analysis of the prototype.

Proof of concept in the digital world has different names, taken from the first two letters of the Greek alphabet: alpha and beta.

- The *alpha test* is the first round of newly developed hardware or software. When the first round of bugs has been ironed out, the product goes into *beta* test with real users.

- The *beta test* usually follows prototyping and concept testing and moves testing out to the users' actual environment for a *real-world* test. The service/product is introduced to a small number of people who are then tasked with trying it out and reporting back any problems to designers and manufacturers.

So *proof of concept* is really a complex and fancy title given to the simplistic task of making sure the market likes your product and that it works – and if not, taking relevant and appropriate action.

MARKETING

Marketing is often misunderstood but, at its best, it is the bridge which connects your product or service to the *market*. It really is an art form, but in terms of business it is the science of communicating the value of your product through its positioning and the way it is presented.

Good marketing can make even a bad product or service sell. Bad marketing can cause the world's most needed product or service to go unheard of.

When looking to grow your business, you need to pay attention to marketing. This covers a wide area, so to make it digestible I have divided it into four sections:

1. Distribution
2. Branding
3. Competitive advantage
4. Social media

Distribution

Distribution – getting your product or service in front of your clients and customers – is a very important but often misunderstood aspect of business. Though it is vital throughout the life of the business, when you are a start up it is a core foundation for growth.

When understood and employed correctly and at the right time, the various elements of distribution that you have at your disposal can generate a return exponentially greater than the cost or effort put into them. Often people think the only method for distributing word about your business – increasing awareness of it – is advertising, but that is only one component.

Let's break up distribution into the *4 Ps*. You can remember them very easily like this:

1. Product – commodity
2. Price – cost
3. Place – channel
4. Promotion – communication

1. Product

This is your physical product or service. All products have their own life cycle that includes growth, maturity and then decline as sales fall.

The route to market comes into play here as you will need to consider how to position the product or service, how to exploit the brand, how to develop the product or service, and the creation of special differentiating features of the product or service.

2. Price

The price is the amount a customer pays for the product or service. Adjusting the price can greatly impact the marketing strategy, and will often affect the demand for the product or service.

In order to set a price it is important to have an idea of the perceived value of the product as well as where you want to position yourself in the market.

In terms of positioning, there are broadly three types of price you can opt for:

- *Premium.* This is a top-end product, e.g. Versace clothes; expensive artwork; Herman Miller designs; Bon Jovi, Elton John or heritage artist concert tickets.
- *Penetration.* This is a lower price to gain market share that then rises, e.g. the strategies used by mobile phone companies.
- *Economy.* This is deliberately at the low end of the scale and is in line with the product itself, e.g. Ryanair.

3. Place

This is where consumers can access your product. This is also known as *route to market*. You may have the best product or service in the world but it will not succeed if you don't put it in front of the right customer in the right way.

By their very nature, products and services in the creative sector are usually discretionary items for consumers. This means they are not like food at the supermarket; people do not have to buy them in order to survive.

So purchases of creative sector products are coming out of a smaller percentage of customers' budgets, as most budgets allocate around 90% to fixed or non-discretionary items (food, shelter, etc.). So how do you catch consumer attention with creative goods and services?

Research is needed here to ensure you achieve the best route to market. The more diverse a company's customer base and product portfolio, and the more competitive its markets, the more challenging it is to design effective and efficient GTM (**g**oods **t**o **m**arket) models.

Here are some helpful questions to ask yourself:

- What are effective strategies to build your first offering, i.e. how will you prepare your product or service to be offered to the market?

- What are the relevant options for routes to market for your business – direct, channel, agency, distribution, licence, self-serve via web/Google AdWords? Evaluate them with pros and cons for each. Consider which brings you closest to your customer.

- Which routes to market enable you to experiment with new product features and product marketing to increase the yield on each new customer?

- Which routes are best for measuring unit profitability?

- Which routes to market enable the best forecasting for scale?

- What is *traction* in your business? How will you know when you have traction and are achieving sales and growth?

- How do you take a product definition and turn it into a development plan?

- How will you demonstrate expertise in acquiring, qualifying and selling to customers in your target market segment?

- Your route to market needs to be tailored to customers who regularly buy in the creative sector:

  - How and where do they shop?

  - Where will they see your product/service?

- You route to market also needs to match your budget and your ability to distribute your product. If your route requires product delivery, for example, look at how much it will cost as well as whether you can achieve it.

Options for routes to market

Here are the different routes to market to consider:

1. Direct selling
2. Selling wholesale
3. Distance selling
4. Online selling
5. Multiple channels

1. Direct selling

Direct selling is where you sell your product straight to the customer, without a middle person, through your own shop or website, door-to-door, using direct marketing or via advertising.

2. Selling wholesale

Selling wholesale is selling your product to a retailer, wholesaler or reseller, who then sells it on to consumers. You usually sell a fairly large amount of product at a lower rate than if you were selling direct.

This is a cost-effective way to shift lots of product in one go and it doesn't use up the resources you would need to approach customers individually yourself.

3. Distance selling

This is where you sell to customers remotely – through a website, telesales or direct mail such as catalogues and brochures. It's much cheaper than renting retail space and you don't have to travel to customers.

4. Online selling

There are different ways to sell your product online, such as through your own website, by using affiliate marketing, through an auction site such as eBay, through a retailer's website, through online adverts, or using direct emailing to a customer database. Selling online saves on costs and it means that you are a global business and permanently open.

5. Multiple channels

Using more than one channel can give you a greater chance of reaching your target. You can work out which channel is most effective and adjust your sales strategy towards that.

4. Promotion

Promotion covers methods of communication that may be utilised to explain the product to consumers, such as advertising, sales promotion, public relations (PR) and personal sales.

Promotion is often mistakenly used instead of the word *marketing*. Promotion includes:

- *Advertising* – the presentation and promotion of a product or service in a paid capacity, e.g. print ad, radio, television, billboard, direct mail, brochure and catalogue, signs, in-store display, poster, cinema ad, internet ad and email.

- *Personal selling* – the process of individually cajoling consumers to purchase a product. Examples include sales presentations, sales meetings, sales training and incentive programmes for intermediary salespeople, samples and telemarketing. It can be face-to-face or via telephone.

- *Sales promotion* – media and non-media marketing communications are employed for a particular time to stimulate market demand or improve product availability. Examples include vouchers, contests or competitions, samples, rebates, trade shows and exhibitions.

- *Public relations* (PR) – a way of increasing interest in a product or service, or creating news and media stories for free. Examples are newspaper and magazine articles/reports, TV and radio presentations, Twitter mentions, press releases, sponsorship deals, exhibitions, conferences, seminars, trade fairs and events, as well as social media.

- *Direct marketing* – allows you to communicate directly with the customer using advertising techniques such as mobile messaging, email, interactive websites, online display ads, fliers, outdoor billboards, etc.

Before promoting your product or service you need to also define what your USP is – this is your *unique selling point*.

USP: unique selling point

Defining your USP means not only working out how your product or service is unique but also how that translates to a hook on which to hang the marketing strategy.

Charles Revson, the famous makeup proprietor from Revlon had an interesting USP. He asserted that he was in the business of *hope*. For a cosmetics company this is intriguing – he was selling products to make women more beautiful, but his USP centred on their mindset, or what he thought was their mindset – the *hope* of becoming more beautiful.

You may have multiple USPs. Take iTunes. It is certainly a unique product in and of itself, but another USP is its *place* (its distribution method, just one click away or less) is so convenient. Also, its price is cheap compared to that for buying a whole album, as customers had to do in the past.

Focus on The Bakery

Whilst there are many accelerators in Britain (structured programmes operated by experts which prepare companies for growth, assist them in gaining finance and offer mentorship), one of the most unique is The Bakery. It is a dedicated tech accelerator for the advertising, marketing and communications industries – so it sits right in the middle of the creative sector.

Headed up by serial entrepreneur and UKTI Dealmaker Andrew Humphries, it is an accelerator with a difference. Whilst most accelerators focus on obtaining funding for their participants, The Bakery focuses on facilitating routes to market for some of Britain's and the world's biggest brands.

Successful *Bakers* will be awarded contracts by the brand's agency, to develop a *go to* market strategy based on their innovative solution to the brand's problem.

The Bakery focuses on obtaining access to markets and income for its attendees, not just investment. This, along with its focus on the creative sector, makes it something well worth investigating.

Andrew Humphries says:

> **❝** There are two elements that are vital to the growth of innovative technology companies; one is access to investment and finance, but sometimes even more important to sustained growth is access to the market and revenues. Many great accelerator programmes exist for the former. The Bakery is the first dedicated programme that offers the world's best advertising and marketing tech developers direct access to and mentoring from top brands and agencies, enabling them to get their technologies into their first big clients quickly. **❞**

www.thebakerylondon.com

Branding

Branding is the practice of creating a name, symbol or design that identifies and differentiates a product.

Having a successful business is not always about being disruptive or doing something new. Hopefully you will at least do it better than others, but even if you don't then branding can step in and help you. Branding at its best is about making your product stand out – even in a market filled with similar items.

Airlines are good examples of this. They are all in direct competition, yet people have ferocious loyalties to one or another airline and certain airline, names – like Virgin, Ryanair and easyJet – conjure up strong feelings in people, both positive and negative.

Branding is not a logo. That is only 1% of it. Just like your own personal reputation, company branding is about what the name represents when people hear it. Branding is the outward presentation – as your personality is to your body, branding is to your business. If you make your brand feel like a friend to people, one that belongs in their lives, you will have a successful business.

Often, especially in fashion, the brand is the actual entrepreneur – e.g. Stella McCartney and Paul Smith. Just as often the creative business becomes larger than life, it can become synonymous with its founder, the very embodiment of them, e.g. Michael Acton Smith from Angry Birds or Daniel Ek from Spotify.

Another slant on this is that the creative entrepreneur's brand can be separate from the product but closely tied with it – look at Steven Spielberg. We do not go to his movies to see him or just because of him – for many of us, if we hear a new Steven Spielberg movie has been released we will go to see it expecting it to be good because he made it.

That expectation is because of the Steven Spielberg brand and what he represents, and the fact this is interwoven into his products. This is rather unique to the creative sector and I think it is because creativity by its very nature is unique, represents passion and is artistic. People grow to trust a brand and they can develop a strong loyalty to creative sector businesses because they become passionate about them.

Even though these products and these creative sector entrepreneurs are producing items which the public can only buy with their discretionary money, they have the ability to conjure up feelings via their marketing which essential, non-discretionary items – such as bread, milk or cooking oil – never can. The ability to evoke such passion is unique to the creative sector.

Here are some tips for branding your company.

Branding tips

- Make sure your branding is *in line with your vision, mission and values*. The brand is the outward manifestation of your vision.

- Get a great *logo*. Place it everywhere.

- Write down your *brand messaging*. What are the key messages you want to communicate about your brand?

- *Be consistent*. Everything coming out of the company should reflect the brand in some way. How you answer your phones, what you or your salespeople wear on sales calls, your email signature, everything.

Look at the broader business sector for a minute and consider some brands which you see every day, such as Starbucks, Costa and Caffè Nero. How are the products of these stores different? Many people would say they are not. The reality is at first glance they are similar. They all serve coffee, they all cost pretty much the same and they are all found on high streets usually within 100 yards of each other.

But if you look closer you will see the following differences:

- *Place*. Some are in more convenient locations than others.

- *Product*. To some, coffee is coffee. Others can tell you their favourite and the subject of these three coffee chains evokes passionate debate.

- *Price*. On this marketing item, the entire major chains are similar or the same.

- *Promotion*. Each has a different brand and some people have an affinity to one brand over another.

Competitive advantage

Another issue to consider when devising your marketing strategy (which is closely interlinked with pitching to find investors) is *competitive advantage*. This is the advantage one business has over another allowing it to generate greater sales margins or retain more market share.

There are many different types of competitive advantage. Understanding the competitive advantage of your product or service is the key to growing your business, as if you don't know how your business or product is different how will anyone else?

Knowing this difference allows you capitalise on it and guard it, making it intangible, difficult to reproduce and sustainable in the long term. Whilst the competitive advantage is more technical than the vision, it should be complementary to it.

As you grow your business and seek to obtain funding, one of the first questions a potential investor will ask is: "What is your competitive edge?" This will tell them if what you have is marketable and hence if it is sellable.

There are several types of competitive advantage but the two main types are *comparative advantage* and *differential advantage*.

1. *Comparative advantage*, or cost advantage, is your ability to produce your goods or service at a lower cost than your competitors and to maintain this low cost base in a way that is difficult for your rivals to undercut.

2. *Differential advantage* is what will be most outwardly noticeable for a creative sector business. This is how you are seen to be different and goes back to the coffee stores discussed above. Given the uniqueness of creative sector businesses this is clearly a major factor to focus on for creative start ups looking to gain an edge.

Innovation strategy for digital media

An *innovation strategy* is important to digital media businesses. The goal here is that through introducing continually better products or services you innovate, protect your business and grow. It is usually employed by digital media companies to *disrupt* the existing marketplace.

The older your business gets and the more it grows, the harder it is to innovate, but the more important it is if you are in digital media. If you are in the business of reality online games, for example, you will need to continually refine and improve the game – as Angry Birds does – or continually improve the service and product offering – as Spotify does. Apple is a notable example of this continual innovation.

Focus on a show business marketing Tsar

Adam Kenwright is managing director and founder of AKA Promotions (**www.akauk.com**). He handles the marketing for some of the world's biggest shows, including *Shrek*, *Dirty Dancing*, *Jersey Boys* and *Billy Elliot*. The agency was founded in 1995 when Adam was 24 and today it is recognised as an innovative, fast-growing, experienced company providing marketing solutions across live entertainment and visual arts.

AKA is a world leader in the marketing and advertising industry with offices in London, Manchester, New York, Sydney and Melbourne.

Adam says:

> **❝** We are the only global agency serving the live entertainment and cultural industries. The principle of our service is simple:
>
> – Create awareness
> – Engage consumers
> – Drive ticket sales and admissions
>
> We work with the best minds in the industry and share our experience and passion for marketing the arts, culture and entertainment. We create imaginative campaigns from a remarkable team based on experience and driven by results. **❞**

The goals of AKA are:

- Imaginative, strategic campaign planning and fulfilment
- Unrivalled box office sales analysis, reporting and recommendations
- Cost-effective and innovative media planning and management
- High-level brand partnerships and sales promotions
- Multi-platform website design and development
- Integrated online strategy, social media engagement and creative advertising placement
- Broadcast creativity from concept to delivery
- Inspiring graphic design and artwork adaptation
- Development and delivery of unique direct marketing and tourism initiatives
- Bespoke merchandise service including design, production and management

Focus on Spotify

As a digital media company which has disrupted the music market, Spotify (**www.spotify.com**) is a great example of marketing success and a company using an alternative route to market for a traditional product.

It is headed by entrepreneur Daniel Ek, who founded his first company in 1997 at the age of 14. With Martin Lorentzon, he set up Spotify in Sweden and in October 2008 the company launched.

Spotify is a commercial music streaming service and has deals with numerous major and independent record labels. Music can be browsed by artist, album, record label, genre or playlist as well as by direct searches. For a modest fee, you can easily access almost any music you wish. There are a number of websites for sharing Spotify playlists and users can rate and discuss songs.

In August 2012 *TIME* reported that Spotify had four million paying subscribers, earning them at least €20 million per month in revenue. Total users reached 20 million by December 2012, with 5 million of them paying monthly. In June 2012, Soundrop became the first Spotify app to attract major funding with a $3 million Series A round from Spotify investor Northzone. Spotify has stated that 70% of its revenue is paid out in royalties.

Their major competition, despite their superior product and easy route to market, lies in their pricing strategy as consumers still illegally download music or watch it on YouTube, which is free. This is a perfect example of how one aspect of the marketing mix can cause you issues even if the others are perfect.

Regardless of this, Daniel Ek has used technology to majorly disrupt the music market and enable a better service. As of 2012 he was ranked 395th on the British Rich List, with a calculated worth of £190m.

Social media

We all know social media is a key enabler these days. It's important to note that the best part about it is that for start up businesses it is a quick and free (usually) way to get noticed and get marketing runs on the board.

With creative sector business social media is a good way to showcase your funky products and services and help to build a *fan base* of people who like your style or product. Loyalty tends to be more sticky for creative products as people generally fall in love with a style of product or service.

Let's have a look at the main social media platforms.

Facebook

You should create a page on Facebook (**www.facebook.com**). I'm not talking about a personal account – I'm sure you have one – but one for business. I suggest keeping personal and business separate.

Offer incentives for customers to join (i.e. the first viewing of your new collection in fashion, for example) and ensure you get a solid number of followers.

The key to maximising Facebook for business is not to have 50,000,000 followers but to have a good number of followers that will buy from you. So you need a *fertile* group and for this you need to fertilise it with offers, incentives and just plain old love – keep your followers engaged through your communication.

LinkedIn

Create a profile at LinkedIn (**www.linkedin.com**). Use it to compile a list of current contacts and to solidify new contacts when you meet them.

So when you meet people, connect with them. We all meet people in life but the key to making them good contacts is to connect with them; follow up with an email, connect to them on LinkedIn, etc. (I call this *marking them as present*); and then stay in touch and play a meaningful role in their lives. Don't just contact them when you need something.

Twitter

Check out Twitter (**www.twitter.com**) and set up a separate account for business. In a similar way to Facebook, you should use Twitter to communicate meaningful things to people.

The key to long-term Twitter success is to use it as a means to keep people close – like friends of your business. Many silly or over-personal Tweets have created crises in the biggest of companies and you need an easy way to prevent this. I suggest a good rule is to tweet whatever you would text a friend of a friend, rather than a friend. This ensures you keep the messages fun, meaningful but not too personal and trivial.

For more advice, contact Twitter expert Mark Shaw (**www.markshaw.biz**).

Flickr

Use Flickr (**www.flickr.com**) to showcase your creative business visually – with pictures of your products and services being enjoyed in all their glory. A picture says a thousand words, so what better form of promotion.

YouTube

Start a YouTube channel (**www.youtube.com**) and upload videos of your products or other areas related to your business. This is a superb way to showcase your business in a longer visual format than Flickr. Whatever area of the creative sector you are in you can use this to really sell.

Google Analytics

Google Analytics (**www.google.co.uk/analytics**) provides vital information about how people are using your website. It enables you to see how many hits you receive and from where. It is like having x-ray vision and gives you the intelligence to shape your marketing message because you start to know who your clients and customers really are.

*

Make sure you understand what each area of social media is; how best to use it for the various elements of your offering; and be aware of why you are using each one (analysing, selling, fostering relationships, etc.).

Each of the above has a different purpose so don't use them ad hoc or only for the sake of saying you have joined them all, but rely on them for your own benefit.

The core of marketing

Marketing is, at its basic core, selling. Selling to your market! Don't forget that.

The marketing process starts as soon as you come up with your creative business idea, because that's your product. It continues when you decide how to price your product *vis a vis* competitors, and it continues further as you work out your distribution channels (route to market). Finally, when you tell customers about your product it becomes essentially promotion – although by that point all elements are in play.

So what does success look like?

This is a question you must always ask yourself to ascertain the outcome you want. It is amazing how many people in business cannot tell you immediately the outcome they want from their business or from certain key aspects of it, such as their marketing strategy.

Remember, these are the essentials:

- *Product* – does it meet the needs of the market?

- *Place* – where will your market find your product, and is this a convenient and appropriate place for the nature of your product and its pricing strategy?

- *Promotion* – will the marketing communications reach the customer? This is your market positioning.

- *Price* – are prices favourable or appropriate? There are many different pricing strategies and the choice of one or the other can position the product well or incorrectly in consumers' minds.

LEGAL TIPS

It is impossible to grow your business without attention to legal detail. I called on top media law firm Gregory Abrams Davidson LLP for some guidance on this area.

Key legal considerations for new business ventures

By Jonathan N. Abrams, Solicitor and Attorney-At-Law, Gregory Abrams Davidson LLP, New York

Congratulations on starting your new business!

This is a general guide – not specific advice tailored to your personal business needs. It is designed to be a resource that helps you navigate the ups, downs, ins and outs that a new venture offers. There is no substitute for taking legal or other professional advice. It will make you look more professional and feel more confident. It should also save you a great deal of time and money in the future, when there is a dispute.

So you have your concept, or product, or website in place. What next?

1. Protecting ideas

Let's start at the beginning: You have an idea. You need to protect that idea.

The legal term for an expression of an idea or concept is intellectual property (IP). IP might be a logo, an invention, a design, a song, or another intellectual creation. IP in a business includes your brand identity and has a value. In some businesses, it is *the* value and needs to be protected by its owner.

Trademarks, patents, copyright and registered designs are all forms of IP protection. Whether you are entitled to receive protection usually depends on availability – for example, whether someone has beaten you to it, or whether you are able to claim that you have the right to IP that has been in the public domain or is public property.

If you are starting out, IP protection may be considered to be a luxury. However, you should ask yourself how integral IP is to your business. If it is essential to protect your idea or brand name, or if there is a risk that you will lose your first mover advantage – and your business model – then the long-term benefits are likely to outweigh the short-term burdens.

As a minimum, I would recommend protecting your brand by registering domain name(s) that you feel are most relevant to your business. Don't forget the alternative suffixes (.co.uk, .com, .net, .co, etc.).

Also be aware that having any registered IP does not guarantee that no one else will use or copy what you have registered. However, being the registered owner permits you to enforce your rights in and to your IP within a legal framework, putting you in a stronger commercial position.

For further reading, I would recommend the Intellectual Property Office website (**www.ipo.gov.uk**).

2. Risk management

Engaging in any business or holding assets through a limited liability entity is generally cleaner and smarter than putting yourself personally on the front line. Thus forming a limited company is a method of self preservation and should always be a consideration for a start up firm.

You will need to weigh up the advantages and disadvantages, such as limited liability, customer perceptions, the extra layer of paperwork, costs in filing and paying advisers and taxes, or the fact that you will be obliged to disclose your company and financial information to the public.

Once again, it would depend on your personal business plans, although in most cases I advise clients to set up a vehicle so that their personal liability is limited.

Aside from forming a limited liability company or partnership, taking out relevant insurance policies can protect your business too. Public and employers' liability policies are the most common and if you allow the public access to your premises, this should also cover occupier's liability. Insurance that is suitable to your business is a must, not a maybe. Find yourself a good broker to help with your risk management.

3. A marriage of equals?

Some entrepreneurs are lucky enough to work with others, perhaps family, friends or ex-colleagues, sharing a common goal in a mutually beneficial arrangement. It might seem like there are many more pressing issues to focus on apart from your agreement with your co-shareholders or partners, but I would not say this is the case.

The idea behind a shareholder or partnership agreement is not to have a daily reference of how to run the business. It most often stays filed away, until the unforeseen happens and you find yourself in a dispute with your partners. This is when the contract between the business owners becomes most useful.

If developed with expert advice, your partnership or shareholder agreement can protect you against future conflicts. Agreements should cover issues such as appointing and removing directors, borrowing levels and issuing or transferring shares.

Crucially, it should limit a shareholder's or partner's ability to compete by using the business's confidential commercial information after they leave and should cover what happens if a shareholder dies or is incapacitated. In fact, it addresses virtually everything that could cause serious conflict in your business in the long term.

4. Put it in writing

If I was paid a pound for every client who has asked about their rights under a verbal agreement, I wouldn't be close to retirement, but I would be a few hundred pounds better off. My advice is always that where there is an agreement, there should be a piece of paper setting out the terms and signed by the parties.

Contracts do not need to be overly long or complicated and do not necessarily require a lawyer's involvement. It can be as simple as a set of basic terms written on a piece of paper, signed by the parties. Email exchanges, where both parties agree on a set of terms, can be argued to be binding, but signatures are always preferable.

Where there is a large sum of money involved, precious cargo, or a very delicate or sensitive matter, detail is key and it is important to take advice from a qualified professional.

If there is an offer from one party, an acceptance from the other, consideration (i.e. money or something of value) changing hands and an intention by both parties to create legal relations, a contractual arrangement between the parties would be implied. There are always exceptions, such as arrangements of a social nature, which are presumed not to be legally binding, where a contract was entered into under duress, or where a set of terms are conditional upon the occurrence of a future event. These presumptions can always be rebutted in court by producing evidence to the contrary.

This *writing* rule applies whether you are dealing with customers, employees, clients, agents, distributors, suppliers, partners or co-shareholders. All agreements should be in writing.

5. The "A" Team

When considering new members of the team early on in business, try to keep your arrangements with them flexible. Flexible work arrangements with *self-employed* staff ensure that you are not paying them for not turning up to work. It also means that you are not tied into a long-term arrangement with people you do not yet know.

Workers sometimes prefer being set up as consultants or independent contractors so that they have more control over their work and schedules. By contrast, employees normally have less control over what they do and how they do it, but will benefit from legal protections that are not available to independent contractors. These include an employee's right to bring a claim of unfair dismissal against their employer. Employees and independent contractors are also treated differently for tax purposes. It is therefore essential that contractors and business owners understand the distinctions so that their legal rights and obligations are clear.

When deciding whether someone is an employee, a tribunal will look for three primary requirements: *control*, *mutuality of obligation* and *personal service*. If any of these are missing, the contract will not be an employment contract. If all are present, all other factors will need to be assessed to conclusively determine whether the facts are consistent with an employment contract.

Make sure that your contracts formalise the working relationship and are clear on their terms, regarding roles, hours and performance targets.

If you take on staff as employees, try to ensure that you are aware of your legal obligations to them. These include statutory allowances, such as sick pay, maternity leave, payroll, holiday allowances and dismissal procedures.

6. On good terms

Ensure your terms of business are specific to your business and watertight. Using generic terms found on the internet will place your business in a vulnerable position as they are unlikely to stand up under scrutiny.

When you are dealing with a client or another business, ensure they are aware of your terms and that yours take priority over theirs. There are also terms that will be implied by law, including consumer regulations, particularly when providing goods or services, so make sure you are familiar with them.

7. Marketing and advertising

The underlying theme with all advertising is to make sure it isn't misleading or advertising anything illegal or illicit. In addition, when creating an advert, make sure there is no association between your brand and a trademark that is not owned by you.

Fine print is key, as it includes specific details about who qualifies for your offer and should ensure you are not misleading or leaving members of the public confused.

8. Premises

A fancy office is no fast track to success and you should think long and hard before wasting valuable start-up funds on leasing expensive premises. Serviced or virtual offices can be just as effective, with lower costs, month-to-month contracts, and no or low break fees. Depending on your business, your own home may be a great place to start – Apple and Google both started out at their founders' homes.

One additional point is that in a slower economy there are deals to be found on commercial or retail property in some areas. Many landlords are open to flexibility if it means extra rent for them. Make sure that your solicitor reviews a lease before committing yourself or your company by signing.

9. Avoid personal guarantees

If you can help it, try to avoid putting your own neck on the line by personally guaranteeing business debts.

10. Keep your customers satisfied

When responding to a customer complaint, my advice is to stop the problem before it gets worse. Take swift action.

11. Handle data with care

If you handle personal information about individuals, you will need to make sure your business fully complies with its obligations under data protection legislation.

Focus on SingOn – a foreign start up

Given Britain's growing creative sector and the fact the UK is the creative capital of the world, many European businesses are looking to establish a second base in the UK to facilitate their global attack.

SingOn is a next-generation singing game service bringing karaoke to the digital age. The concept combines the singing video game (e.g. SingStar) experience with Spotify-like availability, also adding an innovative feature set and game logic to the mix.

The service creates a natural continuum to the digitalisation of entertainment services. Whereas music and movie subscription services (e.g. Spotify, Deezer, Netflix, etc.) have existed in the consumer market for a number of years, the karaoke scene has been struggling to create a solution that combines easy accessibility with the social karaoke experience.

The lack of modern solutions, including the access to large music catalogues and subscription-based business models, has resulted in declining sales in the console singing games business. The current online solutions, on the other hand, still fall short of delivering the core experience of karaoke that users are willing to pay for; service made for TV screen and singers' voices echoing through the speakers. They also still tend to suffer from various usability problems and poor content quality.

Consumers today expect nothing less than easy, on-demand and even free access to high-quality online services, and up to the present the market has still been lacking the success story that could meet these expectations and create sufficient value for the consumer.

Founded in 2009, the Finland-based online media company SingOn has embarked on the quest of offering karaoke lovers the full singing experience. This objective is reached through a multi-platform solution allowing access to the service through connected devices, primarily ones that allow the display of the service on TV screens.

As opposed to console singing games, musical content on SingOn consists of a large catalogue of high-quality cover versions of evergreen classics and the latest hits. Moreover, the gaming element is strongly present in the service, making it appeal to the younger audiences and early adopter consumers. Motivation of consumers is achieved by engaging users to learn, compete and share their performances with friends. Social media integration completes the social aspect of the service, so that besides one's living room, it is also a social activity online.

The service also introduces a highly innovative voice filtering feature to singing enthusiasts. Through utilising the latest audio technology, users can add extra charm to their singing by sounding like their favourite artists.

The service is currently available as a web application and more platforms are to be released. Launched in Finland in 2012 in cooperation with SBS Media Finland, a major radio and TV broadcaster, the service has gained substantial traction in the market, and has already attracted media attention in the European and North American markets.

The company has been selected as one of the most promising start up businesses in several international pitching contests, including the London Tech City UK Entrepreneurs Festival in 2011. The SingOn UK launch will take place in late 2013. As one of the world's largest music markets, the UK represents a highly attractive operating environment for the service.

Being at the interface of the ICT, music and gaming industries, the possible applications of the service are numerous. Similarly, the marketing and distribution network may consist of a variety of actors across industries, taking the form of versatile partnerships. It is these interfaces that best enable innovation, resulting in industry-transforming applications.

This company could be a real game changer and it is brilliant that companies like this are attracted to the UK creative sector for expansion.

www.singon.com

SuperJam

SUPERJAM IS A RANGE OF 100% PURE FRUIT JAMS created by Scottish jam-maker Fraser Doherty. Starting from humble beginnings, the company has gone on to sell millions of jars, has won a variety of awards and is even exhibited in the National Museum of Scotland as an example of an iconic Scottish food brand.

Fraser Doherty started making the preserve in 2003 in his parents' kitchen in Edinburgh. He began with his grandmother's recipe which he adapted to include blueberries and cranberries, and using natural juice as a sweetener instead of sugar. He now sells 40,000 jars a month and has contracts with supermarket giants Waitrose and Tesco.

This is another great example of starting a national business singlehandedly from your spare room.

www.superjam.co.uk

Jimmy's Iced Coffee

THE CONCEPT BEHIND JIMMY'S ICED COFFEE is simple. Jim Cregan had an epiphany after a holiday to Australia; he loved iced coffee and felt there was nowhere in the UK he could find one he thought was decent!

He decided to change that and enlisted his sister Suzie's help. Together they just went for it, in true entrepreneurial style. They soon created Jimmy's Iced Coffee, which you can find in stores around Britain. They sold their first carton in Selfridges, London, on 7 April 2011 and now have listings with Waitrose, Ocado, Welcome Break petrol stations, and delis and cafés across the length of the UK.

Jim says:

> **❝** Doing business in Britain is tough, although doing business anywhere must be pretty tough! We launched our business in a fairly negative time for the economy, but seeing as we sell optimism and not just iced coffee, we turned that frown upside down pretty quick. People need relief from this ridiculous doom and gloom age and we are one epic remedy for that. The three greatest things about doing business are learning, meeting people and steering your own ship. Life would be dull if we didn't and we want to share our journey with anyone who comes onboard. **❞**

www.jimmysicedcoffee.com

CHAPTER 4
FINANCE AND FUNDING

AS YOU START TO GROW YOUR BUSINESS you will no doubt need to take on finance. Whilst this will be less important for fee for service/freelance operators, if you are growing a business it will be needed.

From all the speaking engagements I do and mentoring work I engage in, I can tell you that finance is the area that gets people's blood pressure up the most. It's scary and exciting at the same time, and it's often the only thing people want to talk about. There is a good reason for this – without money you can't grow a business.

Finance can be complex, particularly if you are a creative person and it is not your area of interest in general. So let's take a simple look at it and see how you can ensure your business gets the funding it needs at the correct time. You don't need to become an expert – you just need to understand the key areas.

FINANCIAL RATIOS

Firstly, you need an awareness of the key ratios for financial health. These are imperative for any business plan and are some of the main things banks and often investors will want to know.

Working capital ratio

Assessing the health of a company involves understanding its liquidity – how easily that company can turn assets into cash to pay short-term obligations. The working capital ratio is calculated by dividing current assets by current liabilities.

This is a key indicator of liquidity, cash availability in the coming year and solvency.

Quick ratio

The quick ratio subtracts inventories from current assets, before dividing that figure into liabilities. The idea is to show how well current liabilities are covered by cash and by items with a ready cash value. It is an indicator of the solvency of a company.

Price-to-earnings ratio

Called P/E for short, this ratio reflects investors' assessments of future earnings. You determine the share price of the company's stock and divide it by earnings per share to obtain the P/E ratio.

All publicly quoted companies have readily available P/E ratios which can serve as a benchmark for private companies in the same sector when they wish to sell or exit.

Debt-to-equity ratio

The debt-to-equity ratio is calculated by adding together outstanding long and short-term debt, and dividing it by the book value of shareholders' equity. This shows the proportion of debt for every pound of equity.

If the figure is above 1 it is usually a cause for concern as it demonstrates that the company is largely financed by debt.

Return on equity

Common shareholders want to know how profitable their capital is in the businesses they invest it in. Return on equity is calculated by taking the firm's net earnings (after taxes), subtracting preferred dividends, and dividing the result by common equity in the company.

Gross profit margin

This shows you the proportion of revenue that will be left after taking into account the cost of selling your product or delivering your service.

gross profit margin = (revenue - cost of goods sold)/revenue

FINANCIAL STATEMENTS

The main financial statements you need to know are:

1. *Balance sheet* – shows assets, liabilities and shareholder equity (the worth and value of the business).

2. *Cash flow statement* – shows cash in and out.

3. *Profit and loss statement* – shows profit and loss for a period, usually a year, half year or quarter year.

All sets of accounts have these financial statements and they also have *notes to the accounts*, which are explanatory sentences talking about each key figure.

Let's look at those three types of financial statements in turn.

1. Balance sheet

A balance sheet is made up of current assets & liabilities and non-current assets and liabilities. The determining factor as to whether assets are current or non-current is if they can be liquidated or are due within 12 months.

- *Current assets* include cash, debtors, prepayments, accrued income and stock (if it can be sold within 12 months).

- *Fixed assets* include buildings, land, machinery and computers, as well as intangible assets such as patents, trademarks and domain names.

- *Non-current liabilities*: loans with a repayment term greater than 12 months are the main long-term liability seen on most balance sheets.

The other key aspect is *shareholder equity*. It will either be positive or negative, depending on whether assets or liabilities is greater. Shareholder equity is what the company is worth. This doesn't mean that is what the company would sell for, because it doesn't take into account *goodwill*.

Goodwill is the intangible value placed on the company and it is basically down to negotiation in a private company. Assets might be worth £500,000, but goodwill takes into account your brand, future cash flows, position in the market, ability to be copied, overall market strength, etc.

It is important to generate goodwill and you do it using all the ingredients I have mentioned in this book.

2. Cash flow statement

Cash is king. A lot of people think revenue or assets are king, but the reality is cash is the most important aspect of business.

When we look at our account and it contains a chunk of cash it is easy to be a spendthrift, but it is important to stick to your cash flow and be conservative. Here are some tips:

- *Keep your cash stashed away.* If there is any drop in cash flow you will need to dip into reserves and you always need more than you think you will.

- *Don't tie all your cash up in supplies.* This applies to many businesses but particularly supply-intensive ones like fashion, arts and crafts, and technology. Be careful how you order stock or materials – whilst you need to order enough to meet demand, you don't want cash lying dead in your warehouse. It's very hard to liquidate stock quickly and you almost never get true value in a fast sale.

- *Try and regularise your cash flows.* Some businesses by their nature have seasonal or lumpy cash flows (e.g. fashion is seasonal and art is lumpy). Try to add other arms to the business to ensure a diversity of cash sources and a more consistent flow. For example, the fashion designer may wholesale to stores as well as e-tail and retail; an art dealer may also have an advisory arm earning fees.

- *Always try for cash upfront* or at least within 30 days, even if it means discounting. It will bring you peace of mind and prevent time and energy spent chasing.

- *Always pay suppliers and creditors on time or early.* They will notice that you respect their cash flow which will build the relationship, but it also will mean they are more willing to give you leeway if you need some extra time to pay during the tight months.

3. Profit and loss statement or income statement

The key items here are:

- *Revenue* (total sales).

- *Gross profit.* This is the difference between revenue and the cost of making the item or delivering the service.

- *Gross profit margin.* This formula (shown with the ratios above) will tell you how healthy your production and distribution process is as it shows what you are spending to sell a product. With an ever decreasing margin, a company is heading for the wall. If you earn £200,000 and your cost of goods sold is £100,000, your gross profit margin is a healthy 50%. Each industry has different benchmarks but as a rule if your margin is below 10% you need to look closely at why and assess the business in detail.

- *Cost of goods sold* (COGS). This reveals the cost of selling a product or service and includes direct costs only, such as materials and direct labour costs.

- *Profit* is revenue minus expenses. It is obviously a loss if this figure is negative.

- *Selling, general and administrative expenses* (SG&A). This is the company's operational expenses, such as salaries, rent, travel and utilities.

- *Operating income.* Deducting SG&A from a company's gross profit produces operating income. This figure represents a company's earnings from its normal operations before non-operating income and/or costs (interest expense, taxes and special items).

- *Interest expense.* This is the cost of a company's borrowings.

- *Pre-tax income.* Some companies legally avoid and/or minimise taxes that affect their reported income. Due to this, pre-tax income is usually a more accurate measure of corporate profitability.

- *Special items or extraordinary expenses.* A variety of events can result in extraordinary items. They are commonly identified as restructuring charges or write-offs and should be one-off events.

Understanding financial statements

I have seen many a good pitch fall down because the founder has no idea about these statements. They may not be an area you like, but you must understand them.

There are some common areas relating to these financial statements that cause confusion for businesses and I address these below. I don't want to bore you to tears so I will keep it simple.

- **You can have positive assets and no cash**

  How?

  You will have heard the old expression *asset rich and cash poor*. Basically you can have a lot of assets that are called non-current assets (anything you can't sell or liquidate in a 12-month period) and not so many current assets (cash, receivables, etc.).

- **You can have a predicted profit for the year and still have negative cash flow in some months**

  This is why the cash flow statement is important.

  Just like in our personal finances, some months you will earn and/or spend more than others. The cash flow statement enables you to know when your monthly balance will slip into negative.

  This is important because a lot of people think they will somehow get by, but where will you find the money? You need an overdraft or savings (in business this is called *cash reserves*) to ensure you can get though these months.

- **You can make a loss even if you have positive cash flow each month for the whole year**

  How is this possible?

  You may have to depreciate assets (which is an accounting function only and doesn't affect cash), which reduces profit. This is just one example as to why this may happen.

*

The key to understanding the financial statements lies in:

- Ensuring your company remains solvent. Being solvent means your business remains viable and you stay out of the liquidator's office.

- Knowing what tools you have to play with – i.e. knowing your margins, expenses, etc., is vital.

- Recognising that the statements can tell you in minutes how well your business is performing.

- Remembering they are the window to investors' and bankers' hearts and minds. If your financial statements don't look good or are not presented accurately, loans or investment will be unlikely.

DAY-TO-DAY FINANCE

Here are five things you can put into practice from day-to-day to help you keep ahead of your business' finances.

1. Keep an eye on expenses

Expenses can run away like an out of control train. Make sure that there are proper authorisation procedures in place and watch expenses carefully.

Whilst it is honourable to be a kind person, you are not in business to be a charity. Be charitable to all if you wish after you make a profit, but the business itself needs to be lean and operate in a shrewd manner.

2. Understand accounts receivable

Make sure your payment terms are clear and you have procedures in place to follow up receivables. Many start up businesses have a lot of cash tied up in receivables and whilst they are a current asset, it's not cash until it is in your account.

Many start ups are worried about chasing up money or offending people, but nothing is more offensive than people failing to pay you.

3. Know the sources and applications of your funds

Know the main source of funds (the major clients, etc.) and the major applications of these (your major expenses). Keep a watch on these valuable statistics.

Spend more time on your major clients as it is easier and cheaper to get existing major clients to spend more than to find new ones. Likewise, it is easier to shave a bit off a big expense than to shave a little bit off many expenses if you need to save cash outflow.

4. No one knows your business like you

Regardless of your accountants, mentors and bookkeepers, no one knows or cares for your business like you do. Make it your business to be on top of the financials and make it fun. It should be fun to be in control of your business!

So don't put off understanding the financials. Most people put off what they don't understand, but if after reading this chapter you need further advice, go and get it.

Remember your vision at all times and remember the finances are the key to you delivering on your vision. If the finances stay healthy, you stay on course to deliver your vision and you stay in business.

5. Keep your long-term plan in mind

For many people the long-term plan is to build the business up to sell it in five years to a competitor or in a trade sale or partial sale to a venture capital or private equity company. For others, they just want to have a healthy business that can deliver cash to them over their lifetime so they can live well.

Whatever your personal plan as a shareholder, keep it in mind and direct your actions towards this at all times.

SOURCES OF FUNDING

In this section I will look at the main sources of finance for business.

Family and friends

Family and friends are often the first port of call and they usually can provide you with enough support to get your business off the ground. Even if it's just a couple of thousand pounds, it may be all you need to buy your raw materials, set your website up and cover your upfront admin costs.

There is another key benefit of family and friends funding which is that it augers very well for later attempts to get funding from investors. Whilst it is not a negative not to obtain it – after all, not everyone's family and friends are in a financial position to invest, even if they wish to – it does impress investors who take the view that it is a good sign if your family and friends supported you in the beginning.

After all, it is you they are backing at that early stage, not your business, because early-stage investing is just backing the person's ability to create something. Friends and family funding is a vote of confidence in your ability from those who know you best.

Angels

Angel investors are typically the next avenue after the basic seed capital you have used to get things moving has run out. Angels are private individuals and they typically invest from £10k to about £1m, although the average amount would probably lie between £100k-250k.

Angel investment is not as scientific or as organised as venture capital. Some angels are professional investors, and some are entrepreneurs with a day job who, like me, also want to invest in growing businesses.

Angels bring the following qualities:

- Money
- Propensity to gamble on an early-stage business
- Contacts which are essential to grow your business

Angels can be hands on or off and will often take a board seat or even the chairmanship of your business. It comes down to the individual angel and how they operate.

The percentage stake angels take in businesses varies and is subject to many factors, including the amount needed, the risk and what stage of advancement your business is at. If you are asking an angel to invest in a business which is already operating, it is a different story to investing in one which is just an idea. The more advanced it is, the lower the percentage they will usually take (subject to the amount of funding you are looking for).

An angel may take anywhere from 5% to 50%, but over 50% is unusual as the company then becomes their official legal responsibility. Angels know too that taking control reduces the entrepreneur's incentive and demoralises them.

Focus on an arch angel

Lord Archer, the world famous author, is a professional angel in the creative sector.

Jeffrey Archer is one of the world's most successful authors and has sold over 250 million books. For 35 years, he has captivated audiences with his intriguing characters, ingenious plots and trademark surprise endings. His bestsellers include *Kane & Abel*, *Honour Among Thieves*, *As the Crow Flies*, *False Impression*, *A Prisoner of Birth*, and most recently, *Paths of Glory*. He has also written and staged plays including *The Accused* and *Beyond Reasonable Doubt*.

What is not known to most people is that he has made millions investing in stage productions such as Andrew Lloyd Webber's *The*

Sound Of Music. He had a 35% share in the show, which starred Connie Fisher, who won the part in a prime-time BBC TV series.

He also invested in the West End in *Grease* and *Flashdance*, in the USA in *Hello Dolly* and *Grease on Broadway*, and of course – my favourite investment of his – the regional UK tour of *Dirty Dancing*.

I was invited to meet Lord Archer at his home in London to discuss why he mixes being an author with angel investments in the theatre. I was interested in find out what drives him to operate a separate business solely dedicated to theatrical investment.

His angel activities, whilst borne out of his long-standing passion for theatre, are highly efficient and corporatised in their structure. What's more, over his investment lifespan, his performance and return is positive year on year – something even the best show business producers struggle to achieve.

With this in mind, I was interested in what he looks for. As a passionate art, theatre and literature lover is Lord Archer just looking at solid creative backbone: a great cast, good marketing and a good feel about it? Would he be distracted by the music, a brilliant story or a famous brand?

Lord Archer advised me of the following, which he considers to be of the utmost importance when he reviews proposals for theatrical investments. This can be applied to any creative sector pitch in my view, and is advice to heed well:

- He does not view proposals from anything other than a clear and focused business point of view.

- Track record is important – both of the producer and of the business (the show).

- He turns down nine out of ten proposals because although they may be wonderful shows, they are not investable and do not look likely to deliver a return.

- He believes that creative sector entrepreneurs need to realise that if they are in business the product is essential but the business case remains the key driver.

- His advice to young creative sector entrepreneurs who are looking to set up their own business is simple:

" Entrepreneurs have to realise this is a business. Angels don't want to be giving money away. They want to invest and receive a return so the documents sent to people like me need to show the business case and the potential returns. **"**

www.jeffreyarcher.co.uk

Venture capital

Venture capital (VC) is usually required after your business has gained traction and is looking to seriously expand. VCs will not usually look at early-stage funding – they will come in after seed funding and around the Series A round, and will typically only invest £1m or more.

VCs will bring contacts and money to the table as well as ongoing management assistance. They will not join management but will give their support and experience.

To obtain VC investment you will need to have traction and be generating revenue following a successful proof of concept.

Focus on Octopus

Octopus finds and supports talented individuals and exceptional businesses which focus on investment in people, not just specific sectors. They look for opportunities that are capable of creating, transforming or dominating an industry.

All their investments are UK-focused and they usually invest £250,000 to £5 million in each business, including funds from Octopus Venture Partners. Previous investments include LOVEFiLM, Zoopla, TouchType, Graze and Calastone.

Octopus also does debt-based specialist finance, investing from £1m to £100m in businesses that can dominate their chosen markets or sectors. When considering making an investment, Octopus looks for predictable revenue streams, strong cash flows and asset backing.

The ticketing team at Octopus provides funding to established sports and events businesses. They offer a unique funding solution; providing working capital by purchasing tickets in bulk in advance. Since 2008, Octopus has provided over £250m of funding for sports and entertainment events, ranging from Broadway shows to exhibitions and tickets for top-flight sports teams.

I spoke to George Whitehead of Octopus, who said:

    ff Octopus is one of the most active venture capital funds in the UK, backing companies as diverse as LOVEFiLM, Zoopla, Graze and Swiftkey. I run their Venture Partner programme – a group of around 100 outstanding business leaders and entrepreneurs who co-invest alongside their venture funds and become actively involved with the portfolio. This unique model of bringing A-grade talent to support exceptional business has made Octopus one of the most successful VCs in Europe.

"In my view the UK business scene, particularly around London, is at an interesting tipping point. The credibility of Venture Capitalists in both track record and their ability to write bigger cheques, combined with a new entrepreneurial culture, in part inspired by some of the best entrepreneur and investment tax breaks in the world, has resulted in a thriving funding and entrepreneurial landscape. For Octopus we feel we are at the right place at the right time to have deep pockets and the right connections to build some extraordinary global successes and we are already on track to have been a key part in the creation of what we predict will be billion dollar, game-changing businesses. **JJ**

www.octopusinvestments.com

Focus on Ingenious

Ingenious Investments is an entertainment and media specialist. Over the past ten years, Ingenious Ventures has funded some of the most innovative and dynamic companies in the media and entertainment sectors. These companies have created and run the UK's largest and most successful dance music festival, Creamfields, the *Pop Idol* and *American Idol* TV formats, and the Taste food festivals, where over 50 festivals have been run in 20 cities worldwide, serving over one million visitors.

Here is a summary of how they invest:

> **❝** At the heart of the Ingenious investment approach is the understanding that clients are not necessarily averse to taking risk but that they are particularly sensitive to losses. This subtle, yet important, difference is a key aspect of their investment approach.
>
> "That's why Ingenious believes it is important to align their interests with those of their clients, by investing Ingenious money alongside theirs, using exactly the same funds and investment process. **❞**

www.ingeniousmedia.co.uk

Focus on Passion Capital

Passion Capital is an early-stage investor for digital media and technology companies. It is especially interested in those businesses with global expansion plans and looks specifically at passion and the ability to execute when assessing an entrepreneur's business.

Located in London is Tech City, Passion has backed some digital media and creative sector businesses that have used technology to enable. These include Readmill, Adzuna and LaZook.

www.passioncapital.com

Private equity

Private equity is not dissimilar to venture capital, however it is often for funding above £10m and typically over £100m. Private equity is often associated with leveraged buy outs, management buy outs, mergers and acquisitions by large funds – it will also often utilise debt funding as opposed to straight equity.

As such private equity rarely invests in start up companies, instead favouring established companies with strong cash flows which can grow by integration, corporate restructuring and with a clearly defined exit.

This type of finance is used either as an exit by an entrepreneur or to massively expand their business with an exit in mind. All private equity firms like to exit in two to seven years.

The last decade was dominated by some major private equity activity.

Focus on Oakley Capital

The Oakley Group – owned by one of the UK's richest men Peter Dubens – is an asset management and financial advisory business with over $1 billion of assets under management.

Oakley Capital Private Equity is a mid-market private equity fund with over €280m of committed capital, investing in the UK and Western Europe.

It typically invests in sectors that are growing or where consolidation is taking place. They have interests in performing and under-performing companies, supporting buy and build strategies, rapid growth, or businesses undergoing significant operational or strategic change. Like many private equity companies, they work proactively with their investment management teams, together with other stakeholders, in order to create substantial shareholder value. And then they exit.

Oakley has previously made significant entertainment and digital media investment, including the acquisition of *Time Out* magazine and its subsequent transformation from an old media publication to an e-commerce publishing business.

www.oakleycapital.com

OTHER FUNDING CHANNELS FOR THE CREATIVE SECTOR

Britain is home to some of the world's greatest financing channels. There are some specific channels that are worth noting separately as they can provide you with tangible and practical avenues to achieve your funding needs, from small to large, for start up or growth.

The organisations I cover deal specifically with the creative sector. All too often people in the creative sector feel they do not have specific sources or avenues they can use which understand the nature of their business and the sector as a whole, but here are some that understand the sector inside out.

Start-Up Loans

StartUp Britain and the Department for Business, Innovation and Skills have launched Start-Up Loans. It is a government-backed project that will lend up to £2,500 to young people wanting to start a business with the aim of turbo-charging youth enterprise in the UK.

All information on Start-Up Loans, how to apply, the Start-Up Loans ambassadors and global partners can be found on the Start-Up Loans Facebook page (**www.facebook.com/StartUpLoansUK**) or on the Start-Up Loans website (**www.startuploans.co.uk**).

Start-Up Loans is championed by *Dragons' Den's* James Caan and has so far assisted thousands of entrepreneurs with the seed capital they need to get started.

The criteria to apply for funding are very simple:

- Aged between 18 and 30

- Living in England

- Wondering what it would be like to run your own business

- Not sure about working for someone else

- Wanting to take control of your future

- Keen to have someone help you create a business

- Ready for the real world of business

Lord Young of Graffham, originator of Start-Up Loans, said:

" The Start-Up Loan programme is designed to help you create a business plan, and then give you a loan to get started. You will get continuing support from your mentor, and your future will be in your own hands. The limits of your business will be up to you. **"**

James Caan, Chairman, Start-Up Loans Company, said:

" To be an entrepreneur is more than having a job. It gives you the freedom to make your own mark, in the way in which you choose, and create your own path to success. It can be challenging and exceptionally hard work, but the rewards are immeasurable. **"**

School for Creative Startups Angel Society

Founded in 2012 by former *Dragons' Den* investor Doug Richard, the exclusive School for Creative Startups Angel Society is aimed at business angels and focuses on locating and investing in some of the most promising creative industry start ups, spanning broadcast media, communications, craft, culinary arts, design, digital, fashion, fine art, music, performing arts and beyond.

Events are held across London throughout the year, wherein members enjoy unique access to hand-selected creative start ups for investment opportunities.

I am a founding angel and attended the January 2013 launch of this network at Buckingham Palace, which was hosted by the Duke of York.

The criteria are that you should be looking for investment of up to £150,000 and are a creative sector business.

www.schoolforcreativestartups.com/angel-society

Focus on SEQ Futures

SEQ is a financier to the global sport, music and entertainment industries, with offices in London and Sydney. Clients of SEQ are sport, music and entertainment stars and organisations that need to access future earnings in order to lump sum invest, tax plan, capitalise on immediate investment opportunities, get cash flow for events and tours, upgrade stadium facilities, invest in future talent or manage financial security.

The SEQ team has extensive experience in sport, music, entertainment and financial services, and combines this expertise to assess risk and opportunity.

SEQ's vision is to be the leading, most innovative and dynamic finance house for the industries with which it is involved.

Their clients include:

- Artists, entertainers, sports people

- Player/talent managers

- Player/entertainer associations

- Accounting, legal and wealth management firms

- Corporate sponsors

- Stadiums/venues

- International sport bodies

- Record labels

- Promoters, owners of ongoing events, new event concepts

- Production houses

- Sport and entertainment event marketing firms

- Theatre production organisations

It works by SEQ acquiring at a discount contracted or projected future revenue streams of an athlete, artist, entertainer, or sports or entertainment organisation, on a non-recourse basis.

So given their unique way of investing, they can be a good fit for those with a great concept and strong future bankable cash flow, but limited capital.

www.seqfutures.com

Focus on PROfounders Capital by Oakley Capital

PROfounders Capital is a hybrid early stage investment division under the backing of Oakley's private equity operations and it hits the spot where new and old media merge.

It is a venture capital fund for entrepreneurs. The investors and principals number some of the best-known players within the digital media space – people who have built some of Europe's most successful companies.

The aim is to invest in and support new businesses with capital plus proactive advice and expertise in order to create long-term value and promote entrepreneurism. They believe that the combination of dynamic new entrepreneurs and PROfounders Capital's principals' experience leads to mutual benefits, interesting long-term co-operation and a strong base for new ventures to flourish.

Interestingly for a private equity firm, PROfounders' focus is on early-stage companies operating in the digital media and technology space.

They look for companies that have disciplined and innovative management and which address large potential markets, using technologies that are new or clearly differentiated from any incumbents to generate identifiable revenue streams that can be scaled.

Typically their initial investment will be between £0.5m and £2.5m with the scope and intention to support future financing rounds where necessary and appropriate.

www.profounderscapital.com

HOW TO PITCH FOR AND RAISE MONEY

Pitching for investment is certainly a daunting prospect for most entrepreneurs, especially those in the creative sector who may not have been exposed to financial presentations before.

I have been on both sides of the dragons' den myself, although these days it's usually as an investor. However, as I am still actively engaging in business activities, I also need to engage in large-scale fundraising from time to time – often debt, but sometimes equity.

When I co-developed the Vector Arena in Auckland a few years ago we produced a budgeted cost of around NZ$70m. We certainly had a lot of fundraising to do, which involved debt and equity funding. Eventually we procured close to NZ$60m in debt and the balance was in our and our partner's equity.

I often think that it is easier to raise £1m than £100,000, or £10m than £1m. So for this reason I do not take lightly the trepidation many entrepreneurs face when they approach the process of investment procurement.

For those of you who have watched the TV show *Dragons' Den*, the reality is not altogether dissimilar –although it is usually a little more friendly (acerbic dragons make for good TV after all).

Here are some helpful hints when pitching for funding.

Pitching hints

- *Know your stuff*. Preparation is key, so be ready to answer a wide range of questions.

- *Be clear and direct*. Talk straight to the potential investors and make eye contact with them.

- *Be enthusiastic* (in voice, word and body language) and well presented, but be careful about jokes as they can backfire.

- *Keep your body language congruent with what you are saying*.

- *Keep it simple*, focused and persuade the investor with your arguments.

- *Keep it short and sweet*, around 10 to 20 minutes. Concentration wanders after 20 minutes.

- *Know your targets*. Find out all you can about your potential investors, who they are, what they have invested in and a bit about their company. This is very useful knowledge and helps with the flow of conversation as well as helping you to understand where their questions are coming from.

- *Establish a rapport* and engage in conversation when it is appropriate – don't be a robot. Know enough about your business that when it comes to non-scripted question time you aren't lost for words.

- *Be animated* but don't *spin*.

- *Have clear themes* running through the pitch.

- *Invite questions* from your potential investors.

- *Let the content talk*. Using multimedia in the pitch is a positive, but don't put on a show. Ensure the content is not overshadowed by colour and movement.

- *Bring along one or two members of your team.* Engage them in the presentation and in the questions afterwards. It takes the pressure off you and shows depth and knowledge written your management team.

- *Answer questions clearly* and don't be evasive. If you don't know the answer, commit to checking on it.

- *Be able to explain your valuation.* Going in as a start up asking for £100k and offering 5% is not a negotiating position. It is insulting. That is unless there is a way you can really back up this valuation with strong forward orders, patents in place, etc.

- *Don't stress.* You are talking to people – people who make their money from investing. You both need each other. Your job is just to make yourself irrisistable.

- *Cover the main areas.* Ensure your presentation discusses:

  - Product/service
  - Sector
  - Size of sector (market)
  - People (your team)
  - Financials
  - Proof of concept (traction), if relevant
  - Competitors
  - Competitive advantage
  - Barriers to entry (how easy or hard it is for competitors to copy you)
  - Any protection you have (IP, etc.)
  - Marketing strategy
  - Business strategy
  - Amount being sought
  - Possible exits once the business is built up

The best way to test your presentation and your understanding of the pitch is the *elevator test*. Octopus investments call this the *business card test*. Basically, it means you have to be able to explain what your business is in two minutes (as you would if explaining it to somebody in an elevator) or to write it on the back of a business card.

It is surprising the number of creative entrepreneurs whom I have dealt with who can explain the product and service in fine detail but not the business. You will need to know both for a pitch, but you need to ensure you have a very strong handle on the business itself, as if that is your weakness it will show.

Test your elevator pitch with your friends and the business card pitch on yourself.

Why a pitch may fail

Pitches can fail for several reasons, but if they do it is usually because:

- The potential investor doesn't have faith in the entrepreneur or the team.

- The investor doesn't like the sector, its size or its future.

- The financials do not give the investor confidence or are not in line with their investment or return criteria.

- The business is an idea and not a business.

- The business is a lifestyle business and not one which can grow and scale, or benefit from outside investment or participation.

- The amount of money being sought versus the investment offered is not acceptable to the potential investor.

Why a pitch may succeed

If a pitch succeeds it will be due to:

- Expertise and personality of the entrepreneur.

- The financial return being well received when read in conjunction with the marketing and business strategy.

- Sales potential being solid and distribution channel (route to market) being sound.

- The product or service being unique and difficult to steal or copy.

- The vision for the business being strong and appearing to be in line with the creative sector entrepreneur's demeanour and behaviour.

- Potential exits being available when invested in such a business.

- The entrepreneur's track record with other start ups and exits.

I also suggest trawling the web for investors (particularly angels in the case of a start up) who have invested in businesses like yours. It is much easier to speak to someone who is already interested in your area when pitching.

HOW TO TAKE ON AN INVESTOR AND MANAGE THEM

So you have succeeded in the pitch and you have an investor.

What next?

Getting an investor on board can be like the day after your wedding for some investors. You wake up the in the morning next to someone and you are legally bound. Just as personal relationships, friendships and family have their ups and downs and require ongoing maintenance, business relationships do as well.

What you do next depends a lot on the investor and who they are, along with what discussions you have had with them so far.

I have had many investors in my projects, and in *Dirty Dancing* in particular we had numerous investors in the various productions around the world. I have learned from that and from my own angel investments that communication is the key. If you fail to communicate then you destroy trust. Once trust is gone the relationships is skin with no bones.

I have become displeased and disappointed with entrepreneurs in whom I have invested when they haven't kept me in the loop, failed to tell me bad news or focused solely on their creative passion and neglected the business.

Here are some useful hints for managing the relationship between you and your investor.

Tips for managing the investor relationship

1. Foster the relationship

The relationship is one between two equals, however as the investor has literally invested in you, the onus is on you to keep the relationship flowing.

2. Maintain trust

Always tell the investor bad news immediately. Do not wait, do not hide it and do not sugarcoat it as this makes things worse and loses trust. Tell them the problem and if you need help, ask for it. If not, present the problem and your suggested solution.

3. Report regularly

Even when investors are passive (as they are in show business for example), I like to send reports.

Even with *Dirty Dancing* where we had many investors spread across the globe, we sent weekly reports to keep them in the loop of both quantitative and qualitative matters. This kind of reporting shows focus, professionalism and respect.

4. Keep them passionate

An investor in a creative sector business usually loves the underlying business so don't forget to invite them to exhibitions, show them sample clothes, send them sample music, ask them to look at your designs, etc. You will be surprised how excited even a wily business person can be over this.

This is separate to the money side of things and allows them to stay in touch with the core business and makes it fun for them.

5. Have a clear chain of command

Investors should have one key person to deal with, especially if you have a team which may include a CFO or even an outsourced accountant.

That person should be you. The last thing you want is the investor speaking to other people who may confuse them, or the investor making everyone anxious. If they want any information they can ask you, as an investor would ask the chairman or CEO in a big business, and you can speak to your own people about it and get back to them.

6. Have regular board meetings

Have a board meeting at least once a month. Even if it is only you and the investor there, a board meeting has a formal, professional element to it and you will both be in a different mode than if you were meeting over a casual coffee.

7. Don't waste their time

An investor invests in a business to make a return, so do not necessarily expect them to dedicate hours of their valuable and expensive time. For that you need a mentor.

Some investors may like or want to dedicate time; some may even want paid consultancies. These are exceptions and can be dealt with separately.

I look to be an actively passive investor. I am often on the phone and like to know what's going on, but I don't interfere and save my hard questions for the board meetings. Every investor is different.

8. Have a shareholder agreement

This is the governing information of your relationship, like the constitution of a country. Shareholder agreements are imperative to ensure both parties know where they stand legally. The hope is you will put the agreement in the file and never have to refer to it, but if you have a problem or question, it's good to know it is there.

Business owners should set aside the time to discuss and finalise a shareholders' agreement and both sides should get legal advice. It is not a document to be scrimped on as it may help to avoid the disruption and additional costs likely to be involved in resolving issues in the future.

You also need to think thoroughly about the issues that need to be covered. If you don't know, get a mentor and ask them for advice before you go to the lawyer. This may save money on legal fees if the agreement doesn't touch on a key issue that was overlooked.

A shareholders' agreement only governs its signatories, and there are no rules about what terms shareholders' agreements should include, so advice is key here. If the agreement doesn't mention this it can lead to costly litigation.

In one of my businesses, which I operated with my family, I had many years of litigation costing millions of dollars over a poorly drafted shareholders' agreement, so I know from experience how important it is. The assets were damaged in the process and it was not a productive situation. However, it was one which could have been avoided.

Here are some helpful hints on what to include in a shareholder's agreement.

What to include in a shareholder's agreement

- Transfer of shares
- Approving a change in strategy
- Further fundraising
- Debt raising
- Dispute resolution
- Clarification of key roles
- Clear definitions of key terms
- Definition of core business
- Shareholder information rights and board position rights
- Exit strategy
- Valuation strategy (if one party wants to exit and the other wants to stay)
- Sale of the company
- Part sale of the company
- Sale of material assets
- Board composition
- Voting powers
- Timing of dividend payments
- Issues that may affect the power base of the company, which are potentially contentious

For information about shareholder agreements visit the leading British accounting firm for entrepreneurs: Smith & Williamson (**www.smith.williamson.co.uk**).

Walton Fine Arts

Walton Fine Arts, headed up by art entrepreneur Michael Sakhai and his family, specialises in modern, contemporary pop and street art by original modern European and American artists including Bacon, Banksy, Chagall, Indiana, Lichtenstein, Miro, Moore, Picasso, Warhol and Wesselmann. Walton Fine Arts is also the European agent for the photography of Lawrence Schiller, and Bambi Street Artist's exclusive global agent and source of all Bambi's original art.

Operating from galleries in Knightsbridge, London, Walton is the quintessential creative sector success story – one born out of the founder's passion for art and now operating successfully with a global client base and treasured pieces of art.

There are not many places in London where you can find truly independent family-run galleries selling modern art. For this reason Walton has carved out a solid niche, a successful business and has strong local and international demand.

www.waltonfinearts.com

CHAPTER 5

WHERE TO FIND SUPPORT

IN THIS CHAPTER I WILL LOOK AT ORGANISATIONS in the UK you can go to for assistance, resources and research.

Britain is an entrepreneurial country by nature; it was the home of the industrial revolution and it is where the tech revolution was born. It has always done well in business.

If you are starting your business in Britain, or are one of the many thousands of entrepreneurs who come from abroad and look to Britain as the launch pad or global hub for your business, you will have access to a wealth of support from all corners of the nation. No matter what your budget and regardless of your sector, you will be able to locate research and assistance on any subject.

UK Trade & Investment (UKTI)

UK Trade & Investment is a UK government department working with businesses to ensure their success in international markets and to encourage the best overseas companies to look to the UK as a location for their base.

Its stated aim is to:

> **“** Enhance the competitiveness of companies in Britain through overseas trade and investments; and attract a continuing high level of quality foreign direct investment. **”**

UKTI helps British businesses wanting to gain access to global markets through export, and foreign firms wanting to invest in the UK before expanding globally. With 2,400 staff and advisers, including overseas in British Embassies, High Commissions, consulates and trade offices, as well as business ambassadors who promote the UK internationally and highlight trade and investment opportunities, UKTI provides great support for start up and growing creative sector businesses.

www.ukti.gov.uk

National Association of College and University Entrepreneurs (NACUE)

The National Association of College and University Entrepreneurs is a charity that supports university enterprise by connecting and representing enterprise societies, enterprising students and student entrepreneurs in universities across the UK.

NACUE works with 70 university enterprise societies, supports over 85 universities and assists student-led activities, aiming to ensure that every student in the UK is exposed to enterprise and able to realise entrepreneurship as an achievable and desirable career option. The organisation is working to significantly increase the number of student and graduate ventures, building enterprise skills and contributing to the next generation of entrepreneurs.

NACUE's CEO, Hushpreet Dhaliwal, said:

❝ Peer-led societies today are enablers, increasing the knowledge, skills and networks of students and graduates. They will drive global business success by building more entrepreneurial environments and a culture that enables fellow young entrepreneurs to thrive. **❞**

NACUE delivers mentoring, online tools and resources, and their Leaders Training Conference, designed to train incoming and outgoing presidents of each society. It also runs an annual cycle of events that champion student and graduate enterprise and entrepreneurship. Events include the Student Enterprise Conference, the Varsity Pitch Competition, the Social Enterprise Conference, and various regional events.

I sit on the steering committee for NACUE Create, which is a division aimed specifically at the creative sector of university entrepreneurs.

It is amazing how many university and college students are now considering entrepreneurship as a legitimate post-degree vocation.

www.nacue.com

British Library Business & IP Centre

The British Library Business & IP Centre supports entrepreneurs, inventors and small businesses from start up to launch and then to growth.

Over 300,000 entrepreneurs have used the centre. It offers free access to a huge collection of business IP databases and publications, including general start up advice, information on funding sources, market research, company data, business news and information on patents, trademarks, registered designs and copyright. Other features include:

- Advice sessions with experts

- Workshops & events run by an in-house team and partners

- Webcasts of previous events

- Innovating for Growth programme

I refer a lot of people I mentor to this centre because they also:

- Help inventors and designers to check on the novelty of their ideas when they are considering applying for a patent, registered design or registered trademark

- Help entrepreneurs to find the information they need to develop a business idea

- Support legal professionals in the patent litigation process

- Help service providers to deliver more effective innovation

Visit the British Library website to see a list of the databases you can access through the library (**www.bl.uk/eresources/business/cd-busin.html**). Some of them alone cost thousands of pounds a year for a subscription.

www.bl.uk

Creative Scotland

Creative Scotland is the Scottish national agency for the arts, screen and creative industries, investing money from the Scottish government and the National Lottery towards the development of Scotland's creative future.

A series of investment programmes allow individuals and organisations to apply for financial support to develop their work.

Creative Scotland says:

> **"**We think Scotland's arts, screen and creative industries are worth shouting about. We'll lead the shouting. Visit our Investment Centre to find out how to apply for investment from Creative. We are opening up the arts to a wider, more diverse audience than ever. **"**

Creative Scotland's objectives are:

- To invest in talent
- To invest in quality artistic production
- To invest in audiences, access and participation
- To invest in the cultural economy
- To invest in places and their contribution to a creative Scotland

www.creativescotland.com

Create Wales

Wales is a growing hotbed for creative industries and is used a lot for filmmaking and television production. In Wales this sector provides employment for more than 30,000 people in more than 4,200 enterprises, generating annual turnover of over £1.8 billion.

With a strong film, television, arts and music fabric in the country, Create Wales is prepared to extend support and advice to anyone preparing to start a creative business in the country.

www.wales.com

School for Creative Startups

Dragons' Den star Doug Richard launched the School for Creative Startups.

It provides a subsidised one-year support programme for creative start ups at all stages of development. Be you at the idea stage or already fully active, this programme will teach you how to become a functioning and sustainable business. The School for Creative Startups is a hands-on teaching and support mechanism for early-stage creative businesses during their most vulnerable years, which is when the majority of start ups fail.

I am a *Titan of Industry* at the school and often do mentoring, teaching and speaking there.

The vast array of high profile and high powered Titans to whom students gain access is phenomenal. They include fashion icon Anya Hindmarch, Net a Porter's Natalie Massenet, major Hollywood agency ICM's Pippa Lambert and Sir Paul Smith.

It is a brilliant way to get support.

www.schoolforcreativestartups.com

Enterprise Nation

Run by entrepreneur and StartUp Britain co-founder Emma Jones MBE, Enterprise Nation is a small business support company offering support online, in print and in person.

With a thriving small and start up business community of thousands of businesses around the country, it offers a great opportunity to engage actively with similar entrepreneurs and receive easy to digest advice from a variety of experts in their fields. Regular events are held, great books are published and publications are produced containing practical advice.

The best part is that they are not salespeople. They have no axe to grind unlike many businesses support companies. They receive their revenue from sponsors so their guidance is unfettered advice that you can really trust.

The Enterprise Nation community is dynamic and allows you to provide tips, communicate with other members and experts, and receive quick assistance with your issues or queries.

www.enterprisenation.com

StartUp Britain

StartUp Britain was founded by a group of leading UK entrepreneurs: Emma Jones, Oli Barrett, Michael Hayman, Duncan Cheatle, Raj Day and Lara Morgan. It is a national campaign designed to assist entrepreneurs around the country. Whilst privately run, it also has the backing of the prime minister, the chancellor and the government.

Running events and providing advice in a variety of formats, this sponsor-backed, not-for-profit organisation is an excellent source of information, particularly for pre-opening and start up entrepreneurs.

www.startupbritain.co

British Council's Young Creative Entrepreneur (YCE) Programme

The Young Creative Entrepreneur (YCE) programme is the largest programme of awards celebrating the achievements of young entrepreneurs working within the creative sector. Nine international awards are given annually in the communications, design, fashion, interactive, music, performing arts, publishing, screen and visual arts sectors.

www.creativeconomy.org.uk

Fashion Angel

Specialising in the fashion area, Fashion Angel provides support by way of mentoring and assistance with fundraising. The founder, Alison Lewy has also written a book on these subjects.

www.fashion-angel.co.uk

Tech City

The *Silicon Valley of Europe*, Tech City is a tech cluster based in East London. It is designed to attract the best entrepreneurial minds in the tech and digital media space and is home to many start ups, incubators, funders, accelerators and established companies like Google.

If you are looking to set up, grow globally or scale your business, Tech City is an amazing place to go. It is unrivalled in Europe in its ability to assist start ups or growing businesses in the tech and digital media space.

www.techcityuk.com

Directory

Here is a list of resources for these groups for easy reference.

- Angels Den (**www.angelsden.com**)
- British Library Business & IP Centre (**www.bl.uk/bipc**)
- Business Wales (**business.wales.gov.uk**)
- Business Scotland (**www.business.scotland.gov.uk**)
- Companies House (**www.companieshouse.gov.uk**)
- Creative Entrepreneurship (**creativeconomy.britishcouncil.org**)
- Enterprise Nation (**www.enterprisenation.com**)
- Google Business Solutions (**www.google.co.uk/services**)
- Government information about starting up and running a business in the UK (**www.gov.uk/browse/business**)
- Guardian Small Business Network (**www.guardian.co.uk/small-business-network**)
- HM Revenue & Customs (**www.hmrc.gov.uk**)
- IdeasTap (**www.ideastap.com**)
- London Business Angels (**www.lbangels.co.uk**)
- NACUE – Create (**create.nacue.com**)
- School for Creative Startups (**www.schoolforcreativestartups.com**)
- Scottish Enterprise (**www.scottish-enterprise.com/fund-your-business**)
- Smarta business support (**www.smarta.co.uk**)
- StartUp Britain (**www.startupbritain.co**)
- Start-Up Loans (**www.startupbritain.co**)
- UK Business Angels Association (**www.ukbusinessangelsassociation.org.uk**)
- UK Trade & Investment (**www.ukti.gov.uk**)

ACCELERATORS

There are many accelerators who can help expand your business. Here is a showcase of some of them.

TechStars London

Formerly known as Springboard, a recent merger led this to become TechStars London, a JV with the famous TechStars USA who have their own TV programme.

David Cohen, CEO and founder of TechStars, has given the city a very warm welcome:

> **"** We've had our eye on the burgeoning London tech scene for some time, well aware the US doesn't have a monopoly on either tech skills or entrepreneurship. The current business climate here means we can work with an incredibly broad spectrum of British and international teams and top talent. Merging with Springboard will allow TechStars to deliver great results both for start-ups and investors. **"**

TechStars London is run and jointly owned by Jon Bradford, former proprietor of Springboard (for whom I have had the pleasure of acting as a mentor).

www.techstarslondon.com

Accelerator Academy

I was fortunate to be a founding mentor for the Accelerator Academy run by Ian Merricks of White Horse Capital (**www.whitehorsecapital.co.uk**). The Accelerator Academy enables ambitious early stage and start-up entrepreneurs to build better businesses faster, increasing their appeal to investors.

The Accelerator Academy and planned accompanying Accelerator Fund provide expert training, mentoring and access to capital for the businesses developed.

Accepted applicants receive the following:

- 150 hours of training, mentoring and support, with weekly classroom sessions and workshops, fortnightly Accelerator Clinics, weekly mentoring from a dedicated personal business mentor (all exited tech entrepreneurs) and attendance at other start up and accelerator events.

- Access to over £150k of offers, discounts and deals from a range of partners, reflecting their position as a tier one accelerator.

- Intensive, structured support with team, market and investor readiness.

- Discounted and fixed-fee legal and accounting services from sponsors.

- Admittance to the Accelerator Academy Alumni network (upon successfully completing the programme).

- The opportunity to present to key early-stage investors at the end of the programme.

Backed by some marvellous sponsors, Accelerator Academy is a unique Accelerator operated weekly, so it therefore allows start up entrepreneurs to combine it with actually building their business.

www.acceleratoracademy.com

Wayra Academy

Wayra is Telefónica's seed-stage start up funding firm, launched in April 2011. It provides financing, mentoring, access to technology expertise within Telefónica and use of purpose-built Wayra Academies.

Successful projects initially spend six months in a Wayra Academy, receiving help to accelerate their business and technical support to further develop their ideas.

www.wayra.org

Soleil d'Or

Soleil d'Or is a high jewellery society that provides access to high jewellery and philanthropy.

Their collection is vintage, contemporary, bespoke high jewellery and timepieces from established high jewellery ateliers and private collections. Each piece carries a unique story. *Soleil d'Or* manages all administration of security, logistics and insurance matters as part of the paid-for service.

The members also receive invitations to exclusive events. Centred on high jewellery, these unique and informal gatherings offer an opportunity to experience exquisite pieces and develop knowledge, enjoyment and appreciation. Other member benefits include the Soleil d'Or concierge service, which provides every conceivable lifestyle support.

www.soleildor.co.uk

Myriam Blundell

Myriam Blundell_Projects is a London-based art production company founded in 2004 that showcases experimental and creative forms of displaying visual and performing arts. They work with a variety of mediums, ranging from film, photography, installations and live art performances to contemporary music and dance. What makes them unique is the focus upon new and unusual ways of approaching the conventional to create new forms of display and engagement with contemporary art.

MBP curates and produces a wide range of art events, including live art events, commercial shows and institutional exhibitions in the UK and abroad. The practice provides visual and performance content to a variety of public and private art institutions through the staging of events designed to fit alternative spaces, displacing art from the conventional gallery environment to reach a wider public viewing audience.

MBP also operates a residency programme which provides emerging and mid-career artists with the opportunity to live and work in the South of France. The programme is designed as a creative incubator for nurturing innovative ideas, new encounters and unique exchanges across diverse art mediums, aimed at enhancing its residents' creativity and personal and professional growth.

www.myriamblundell.com

CHAPTER 6

PSYCHOLOGICAL MASTERY

IN BUSINESS, PSYCHOLOGY, HEALTH AND ENERGY are just as crucial as any business idea and concept. As entrepreneurs who are building businesses, you are creating something tangible from something intangible. Energy is the fuel we need to live but also to create and build. You don't see many unfit, fatigued, lethargic entrepreneurs. Those who become that way often suffer heart attacks and die at an early age. The statistics on early heart attacks for stressed businesspeople are unbelievable!

I'm not here to tell you what to eat or be a fitness or life coach, but I am telling you that staying healthy, fit and having the right mindset will contribute 50% towards building your business successfully.

In business staying power is everything. Business can be hard, test your patience and test your self belief. It is easy to be dragged into a stress reaction and become negative. Warren Buffett once said that "Risk comes from not knowing what you are doing." I also believe stress comes from the same place.

Stress is a real physical condition created by an illusion – the illusion of fear of an outcome that may never eventuate. Physiologically stress comes from the *fight or flight* response. The body releases adrenaline and stress hormones to mobilise our body to fight or run fast, and literally shuts down non-imperative systems including the immune system and digestion, to preserve energy for the fighting or running.

If you think this is boring or not important, to stop reading now would be a mistake. Stress kills! It damages your body and can ruin your health and the quality of your life. I have learned that stress in business is futile and when looking back at things I was worked up I cannot even remember why in most cases.

As Bruce Lipton says in the *Biology of Belief*: "Unlike competitive athletes, the stresses in our bodies are not released from the pressures generated from our chronic fears and concerns." So for businesspeople, a build up of stress is even more of an issue.

Once I was speaking about this at an event and a gentleman in the audience accused me of talking voodoo business.

I respected his opinion. However, to ignore these ways to give yourself more energy and health for building your business is to choose negativity and stress, which in my view is not a good choice. So if meditation is not your thing, if you're too busy trying to start up and hold down a job whilst looking after a family, or you just don't know where to start, here are some techniques that everyone can use.

TIPS FOR PSYCHOLOGICAL MASTERY

1. Stay positive and passionate

The Mayo institute in the USA undertook a study which showed that positive people live longer. In the study, researchers found that a pessimistic group of patients had a 19% increase in the risk of death when comparing their expected life span with their actual life.

Our health is inextricably linked with our mindset, so if you are in business you have to stay positive. Athletes have known this for centuries, so they avoid the negativity by thinking positive, visualising their results and remaining passionate.

Staying positive does not mean having your head in the sand. It means choosing how you respond to stressful circumstances and consciously making the choice to take the lighter and higher positive road. It may not happen all the time but if you achieve it 51% of the time you are achieving a good result.

A lot of positivity comes from being passionate about what you do. If you are passionate about what you do you have focus and clarity. You release strong serotonin (the happy hormone) and literally move yourself into feeling good and being in good health.

Negativity of family and friends

In the creative sector I often see families and friends of creative businesspeople acting as **negative reinforcers**, nay saying the entrepreneur's goal of starting or growing a business and dismissing it as merely a dream. "Oh this is too risky, don't quit your day job," they say. Or, "This is not responsible when you have a family," and "You should be getting a job after university and getting experience."

What you need is not sage advice, but unwavering support!

The creative sector in the UK accounts for 1.5m jobs and in the euro zone 8.5m. This means that:

(**a**) Many people are working in this sector

and

(**b**) Someone is employing them, i.e. an entrepreneur or a company started by an entrepreneur.

Why can't this be you?

Tom Rath and Donald Clifton pioneers of the field of positive psychology, wrote about this in their book *How Full is Your Bucket?* having studied millions of people around the world. It's centred on others filling up your bucket or dipping into it and looks at how daily interactions with people do one or the other. Being aware of this concept is vital to staying positive and to keeping energetic.

Who knew that mental work or anything where you draw on your emotions (as opposed to physical work) burns energy by the truckload? We all know how drained we feel after a day of mental work, studying or an argument with a draining person.

Fortunately most creative sector entrepreneurs are obsessively passionate about their creations and the businesses they build around their creative passion. It is important to stay this way.

2. Time management

After health, *time* is the most precious resource, not money. We can always earn more money but we will never get more time. And if we don't work actively on our health the time we do have can deteriorate.

Too many people waste time in business and don't value their own personal time. They also don't recognise it is a resource. If you waste just one hour a day you have lost a whole day of your life each month – that is a travesty in my opinion.

Working 9 to 5 and sitting at a desk all day is a waste of time. Most people are productive for only half that time, or less, yet the *machine* dictates they must stay at their desk, have one hour for lunch each day and four weeks holiday each year.

Don't feel guilty if you work 20 hours a day and don't feel guilty if you work two hours a day. As long as you are being productive and making the best use of your time then you are achieving your goal. Working hard and long doesn't mean you are achieving more. There is a time and a place for that but it is not necessary all the time. Often I work two hours a day and achieve more in that time (productivity wise) than I do if I sit at my desk for 15 hours.

Master your own use of time. Be efficient. Do more in less time and leave time to innovate, to dream and to visualise. This is when you will really improve your business growth as innovation is the lifeblood of any growing business.

Some days I feel like working all day and I am productive. On other days nothing seems to flow so I just spend the day having coffee, walking and enjoying the day.

The worst use of time is to become controlled by others. In your office if you spend time replying to emails when it suits others, take calls all day and run around like a mad person you lose control of your own time, waste a lot of hours and do not work on the business, just *in* the business.

Mike Duke, CEO of American retailer and the world's largest company Walmart, is well known as *the king of time management*. Check this out:

- Mike Duke runs the world's biggest company.

- He oversees 8,600 stores.

- He has a staff of 2.1 million people.

- Yet he still handles all his emails by the end of each day.

- He is so dedicated to sticking to his schedule that he is not above standing up to leave while people are still talking to him in meetings.

- He has numerous time management systems in use, including this one:

Duke has eight senior people reporting directly to him. On the cabinet near his desk, he has one folder for each of them. It has their name and the time of Duke's next meeting with them. Before they arrive, he takes out their folder and reviews all the areas they manage. Anything they have promised to do is listed in the folder too, so he keeps that item in there until it's done. This means he concentrates on the eight people who can create the most change in the company. (Most leaders have a far wider focus.)

He prepares for each meeting before the person arrives. He is clear at all times what and where they are up to. Most CEOs of big companies have only a vague idea. He follows up rigorously. Most senior managers have no system for follow up. Even at Walmart, where efficiency is an obsession, senior staff marvel at how much Mike Duke gets done with this system.

Another great book on time management is *Dare to Prepare* by US Attorney Ron Schapiro (one of America's top trial lawyers). He outlines how preparation has made him the major success he is in law and business. He puts his competitive advantage down to having his *ducks in a row* before his work.

The reality is, people who get to the top in business aren't necessarily smarter than their competition. However, like Mike Duke they are usually more focused and organised. I am obsessed myself with managing time in business and personally.

3. Ongoing education

Ongoing education is a key component in business psychology. I read books on business, personal development and physiology. I attend courses and I study almost constantly.

Education, in whatever form suits you best, is imperative. This is what sets you apart from others and will give you the improving knowledge to grow and successfully operate your business, maintain your competitive advantage and have fun in the process. After all, if you are passionate about your business then ongoing education will be a pleasure.

Study whatever appeals to you. I don't suggest you go out and do a course just to have the letters next to your name. Do whatever it is that makes you happy and helps you develop as this will enable you to develop your business.

4. Understand yourself

Each of us has a different personality. There are known to be over ten personality types and each has different traits, .

Find out as much as you can about yourself. Once you know yourself and your personality, you can try to change what you don't like or that which does not serve you. Enhance what you do like and accept everything else.

Clearly people's different personalities mean they react differently to different circumstances. By knowing this you can manage your reactions better.

5. Model others

In spite of the fact we are stuck with some aspects of our personality, in a physiological sense we can model the behaviours of others and their success. Modelling is about studying and recreating the excellence of someone else and achieving something that someone else has by modelling how they acted in going about it.

I have modelled a lot of successful people. Modelling is about not only studying people but working out how they think and modelling that thinking with regards to your business. If you want to be a successful internet entrepreneur, you may model Steve Jobs. For an example of a successful TV producer maybe look at Simon Cowell, or for a successful fashion retailer look to Sir Philip Green.

Modelling is about observing and then applying the behavioural traits to yourself, until they become subconsciously part of your behaviour. Just like learning to drive, ski, ride a horse or a bike.

6. Energy and health

Without energy none of the world's great entrepreneurs would have achieved all that they have. Take a look at them; Google them and witness their habits. Many are fitness fanatics. A lot don't drink alcohol and most of them get up early.

I'm not saying these people are superior to others who make different choices. What I am saying is that Bill Gates, Sir Philip Green and Mark Zuckerberg do not have more hours in the day than you or me. What they do have is more energy than most of us. Steve Jobs died so young, yet he achieved more in his life than most people, even more than other successful entrepreneurs might achieve in ten lifetimes.

Maintaining energy levels means different things for different people. Work out how to achieve your optimum levels of health and whatever makes you feel good for the longer term, and follow that path.

Having more energy will give you the best chance of not only enjoying your life but it will also give you the energy you need to build your business, grow it and take a positive attitude towards any issues.

How many of you remember feeling sick or tired and being presented with a problem? The same problem presented on another day when you feel well is often not a problem at all. So get into your optimum mindset and level of fitness, and try to stay there.

Human Performance Institute

The world famous Human Performance Institute trains business leaders, executives and global entrepreneurs to create what they call corporate athletes. Their whole vision is centred around "offering solutions that help business executives and employees expand and manage their energy for increased performance, even under intense pressure."

They say:

> **&&** For decades, the Human Performance Institute has believed that employee engagement is directly linked to employee health. Essentially, that the body is business relevant, from muscle to mind. By studying the needs and behaviours of elite performers, the Institute was able to provide groundbreaking insight on how to prepare business executives to achieve unprecedented performance levels. **77**

7. Clear thinking

You need to be able to state in three simple points:

- The biggest positives of your business

- The greatest weaknesses

- Your top three priorities for the month

This kind of clear thinking helps get your priorities right and keeps these key business elements at the front of your mind so you don't lose track of them.

8. Be flexible

You need to be flexible at the same time as having a clear idea of where you are going. Top business leaders have a clear vision but are flexible enough to change their methods midstream. Business and the world as a whole is dynamic so you can change your strategy, but be true to your vision and mission.

If you try something and get a result that you don't want (which some might call a failure), you need to try something else. This is particularly important in the start up phase.

Some people think that it's worth taking the fight to the streets and that true entrepreneurs just keep trying and trying for 20 years until they get their break. I think that's a waste of time and you need traction in 20 months, not 20 years.

Steve Jobs wanted to dominate the tech market. Did he envisage that in doing this he would become a game changer in the music industry? I doubt it. However in order to dominate the tech world he needed to revolutionise other sectors. This is an interesting concept I think.

9. Go the other way

John Kay, the British author of *Obliquity* says: "If you want to go in one direction, the best route may involve going in the other." Paradoxical as it sounds, goals are more likely to be achieved when pursued indirectly. So the most profitable companies are not the most profit-oriented and the happiest people are not those who make happiness their main aim.

This means making time to innovate your business, not just sitting tearing your hair out, thinking how you can make more money to meet this month's bills or payroll. If that is what you think about all the time you may not get it. Go the other way – have fun, focus on your vision and run your business well – this is the way to success and then financial reward.

10. Health at your desk

If you are going to be spending hours at your desk crouched over, or long periods standing up every day, you need to know how to keep yourself fit and healthy.

Believe it or not sitting at your desk all day typing and staring at the screen is pretty dangerous. I'm not joking! It stresses the joints, fatigues your muscles and damages your eyes. Going to the gym twice a week might keep you looking good but won't necessarily keep you injury free.

Take a look at any top performing entrepreneurs and you will see that most are in tip top shape, stay active and live a healthy lifestyle. The decade of the long, alcohol-fuelled lunches and out of condition bodies chained to desks has gone.

Developing this tenth point further, I will now move on to look at fitness and psychology.

FITNESS AND PSYCHOLOGY

I'm no fitness trainer and I do not have a six-pack, but I have learned that to progress in business and to maximise our innovative capacity, we need to operate at near optimum level in our body and mind at all times. Most people operate well below optimum every day of their lives, but if you want to grow a business this is not good enough to get you through.

In the creative sector we also use our body in funny ways. If you are on your feet all day or use your hands or just sit on your bum all day, you are not using your body as it should be used. Unfortunately evolution is millennia behind how we use our bodies. If you can avoid health problems associated with your job you will literally have a better quality of life, a better mindset and be much more efficient and achieve more.

Paul Manley is a physical therapist in London who specialises in treating people in the creative industries. Having treated over 30,000 patients in 30 years, he knows how to help people avoid problems as well as how to treat them. Paul says this about getting your body in what I call *business ready shape*:

> **“** Fear is the main factor. Fear is bred by uncertainty. People react very differently to uncertainty, ranging from the *head in the sand* approach to the screaming Banshee approach, from the stoic masochist to the suicidal maniac. This is when it is vital that the employee knows as much as possible about their condition, its causes, cures and above all, its prognosis. This is where my sort of expertise comes into its own. I have found that the very act of filling my public RSI survey has resulted in people realising not only their bad habits, but also being able to identify the very specific areas of their anatomy, and understanding why it is in pain. Knowledge is power, power negates anxiety.
>
> So pay attention to your body, give it the respect it deserves. **”**

Paul's tips for keeping your body in the necessary shape to carry on your creative sector business are:

1. Use varied means of communicating with your computer – keyboard shortcuts, pen tablets, voice recognition, etc.

2. Do not use the scroll wheel on your mouse; this will create pain along the top of the forearm.

3. Don't grip the mouse when you don't have to.

4. Experiment with different mouse types and sizes. Always use a laser, wireless mouse.

5. Do not hold the hands pointing up or the extensors will become tired and ache.

6. Stretch the hand and forearm tendons regularly.

7. Vitamin and mineral supplements are useful, depending on the lack of these elements in the individual. Vitamin B12 and magnesium can be very useful for the run-down person or those prone to cramp. Certain muscle building dietary supplements can help to build muscle where a person has poor muscle development.

8. Cardiovascular exercises stimulate blood flow to the whole body and are therefore beneficial to all the muscles.

9. Air conditioning drafts should be avoided for those of us who are sensitive to such things. Cold air will make the highly temperature sensitive muscles of the neck and the deep muscles of the forearm contract in tension.

10. Hydration. Without water we would all be dead in three days. Water is the largest element of muscle and is fundamental to all functions of the body. An adult should consume around 1.5 litres per day.

11. Sleep is one of the most important factors of all in recovery. It is more than mere rest; it rebuilds us nightly and is to be greatly respected.

12. Avoid texting, gaming and emailing by phone.

13. Arms on chairs should be used. The desk design should not prevent the operator from getting close enough to their desk. Ideally one should be able, with the base of the spine touching the back of your seat, to get close enough under the desk to touch your belly to the desk edge. Too many desks don't allow for this. If this is the case, the operator will be forced to sit forwards on the edge of their chair. This is very bad for posture and circulation to the legs.

14. Footrests are vital for the vertically challenged.

15. Monitors should be placed so that the operator's natural eye line falls near to the top of the screen. The screen should be angled slightly back at the top so that it is parallel with the operator's face-line.

Focus on creative sector entrepreneur Paul Manley

As mentioned, Paul's focus is on the creative sector. Whilst he sees clients from all walks of life, he sees many musicians, singers, dancers, performers, art and craft makers, artists and chained-to-the-desk creative and digital media businesspeople.

He also decided he wanted to get into business and given his experiences with creative sector entrepreneurs, his own business desires and his tech knowledge, he launched a start up. In fact he launched *three*. Paul said:

❝ Around the tenth year in practice I realised that I would never be a wealthy man if all I did was help people out of pain – my profession is a vocation, not a business. So I asked a patient of mine whom I adjudged to be successful what the secret was to making lots of cash. He immediately replied 'Paul, you need a widget!'

What is a widget I asked? 'It is something which you devise, modify or invent which can be produced and distributed by other people and you keep the profit,' he replied.

So, I determined that I must create a widget. I had many ideas for inventions and was good at solving riddles and modifying and fixing things, such as people and washing machines, so I allowed the creative juices to mature. Whilst typing one day I noticed the discomfort that I continually suffered in my forearms, shoulder and neck. Pins and needles were commonly experienced.

I started to design something to alleviate the problem. After all, I had been advising and assessing both musicians' playing techniques and office workers, so I should be able to devise an aid. Thus was born The Tendaguard wrist rest. The strapline read 'Forget the rest, this rest is best'.

It took 18 months to learn about materials, manufacturing processes and their costs. I also studied *The Guerrilla Marketer's Handbook*, which was a first dip into the realm of business and served me very well. I learned that businesses will often be let down by their frontline sales staff.

I designed the unit, making certain that I could assemble the prototypes at home at each step, modifying materials, dimensions and the assembly process. After 16 months we were ready to produce up to 500 units per week. I had learned about price positioning and decided that £27.50 was about right. The wrist rests were luxurious and hardy, and the market price range with similar products was from £5 to £45. My product was superior to the highest priced similar product. We were contacted by a huge investment house and won an order for 2,000 units against stiff competition.

The next lesson was a harsh one. I learned that the huge companies can have exclusive supply and delivery contracts with third-party companies. This cut into my profit. Throughout this period I had to learn a lot of things and I would encourage anyone to learn,

learn, learn. If you don't know how to do something important to your progress, whether it be materially, mentally, creatively or spiritually, then learn about it.

The internet opened before my eyes soon after it first started. I had an immediate, intense craving to create websites. A new medium was born; the freedom of the individual to produce his own business was global. Finally I might be able to use this medium to produce my interactive anatomy project. It wasn't ready then, but in five years the technology had caught up with my idea and my first anatomy website was created. This, not surprisingly, brought me business and much acclaim – people loved it.

My most recent project has been developing the world's first truly online RSI Assessment process (**www.rsiassessment.com**). This used a combination of all my realms of knowledge – clinical, business and website coder. I have had to learn about server administration, amongst many other things, to get it all working the way I want it in all its minutiae.

In conclusion, it is a curious phenomenon that life's pathways often proceed towards a single point, that point being the result of many talents and realms of expertise. I urge you all to follow your dreams and to make the most use of your existing abilities to succeed. Where you don't have abilities which are necessary, learn them. Our minds are capable of much more than we think. **"**

Focus on Amanda McGregor

Amanda McGregor is a visionary, skilled in development and communications, who has used her creativity to help start ups and growing businesses.

Working with many large corporate and small business owners seeking a unique, cost-effective way to brainstorm, she has assembled a successful business in London. I asked her how she works.

❝ I like my consultations and development programmes to feel enlightening. The unusual way I work is largely blind to normal business conversation, in that I psychically tune in to the region of the client's soul energy field, which is informative on security and development. I see the detail of how stable their energies are and how the different energetic emotive skills of the client collaborate. I then use vision and channel from the universal body of consciousness and inner communication of the body to build and strengthen constructive foundations for growth and high performance. I consider the enhancement of clear vision to be a primary manifestation tool to create a product or service.

When checking the balance of a person's energetic stability I look at the nature of the energy field to channel positive intention with the creation of security, strategy, infrastructure, project, partnership, foundation, support and communications. Looking at the energies surrounding the situation as far as interference and emotive energies are concerned often reveals hidden agendas from other parties that need to be aligned to streamline direction or placing. I look at all relevant persons working in their aligned skill sets.

I try to be clear as to how individuals perform best in certain roles. I also look for thermals or bodies of energy that enhance growth and that are natural to riding waves of positive collective consciousness when aligned.

By asking for feedback from the client I create a space that enables us to work together with healing, channelling and soul development to bring alignment to direction, to change personal energy patterns, and to bring stability and consistency to all aspects of life. We develop creative vision, services and products to bring a high level of clean and direct communication to the market. Most clients feel stress free working with me; they are consciously light and in a position to manifest change consistently and productively. The overall feedback I receive is generally congruent to stable positive experience and delivery. **"**

Here are some words from a small business entrepreneur in the creative sector who has worked with Amanda:

" Amanda's skill in thinking with words and outside the box has given me the opportunity to view my work in a different light. She uses suggestion in view of the whole song, looking at the message. By having me change a few words within the body of the songs they came alive, creating a whole new vibe in what I was doing. She has catalysed my inspiration. In the last two months I have written eight new songs I am so proud of and they will be recorded on my up-and-coming solo album. Releasing my thoughts into a different space has given me a greater understanding of storytelling in a few lines and enables me to sing the songs with more feeling and openness than I ever thought possible. **"**

Tim Balmford, singer-songwriter

I do not know how it works, but what I can tell you is that Amanda's sessions have helped me to unlock my creativity at times when I needed it. We all have to draw on whatever works for us and all avenues are well worth a try to allow our creations to mould seamlessly into business, free of obstruction.

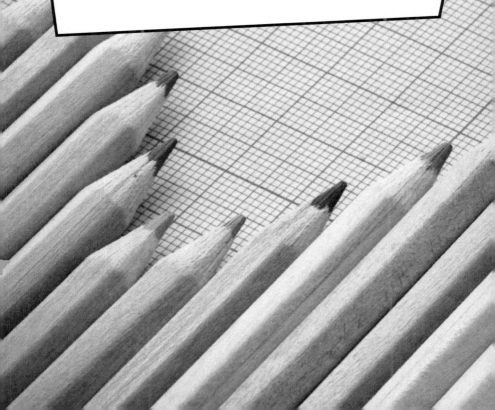

CHAPTER 7

WHAT TO DO NEXT

HAVING READ THIS FAR YOU NOW HAVE the key ingredients to start and grow a business, fund it and get it off the ground. It is important that you next work out how to integrate your business with your life.

Many people I have spoken to or mentored come to me with great business ideas already well thought out, but they just can't transition from theory to practice. Even people who have launched one or more businesses before suffer from this. It can become like stage fright.

Don't get stuck in the theory! There is never a *perfect* time to make the leap. You should make it as soon as you feel only a little uncomfortable about it because if you wait until you feel completely comfortable then get ready for a lifelong wait.

This chapter explains how to cross the bridge and take your business live.

COMBINING IT WITH YOUR JOB

When planning to set up and launch your creative business, it is not necessary to give up your day job. Having a stable income is useful and provided you are not compromising your work there is no reason why you can't do both until your own business reaches a critical mass where it can stand on its own.

Get the right day job

For many creative sector entrepreneurs, their job is often in the same area as their creative business. Maybe you work part-time as a musician, singer, backstage crew in a theatre, teaching art and craft classes, in a store if you love fashion, or coding if you love digital media. Clearly any job you have is good as long as you enjoy it and it pays you well, however it is better to have a job in the area in which you want to be in business.

If you want to have a fashion business, get a job in a clothing store. If you want to design, get a job in a furniture store, for example. We get inspiration and ideas from our environment so you are more likely to get ideas for your business when working in an area which is related to your area of interest than if you are working, say, in a factory that is totally unrelated.

Choose carefully so that you manifest your new business from what you do or see each day. Also, in this case your boss is likely to be more understanding of your business and may even offer their help or mentorship.

How do I find time and energy?

If you have a day job it probably takes up the whole day. Even if you work in a fashion store and are a designer, you may be working from 9am to 6pm. When do you get time to dream, let alone time to do the administration and strategic tasks I have discussed? It's all about time and energy management.

Undertake research

Read everything you can get your hands on: that is all publications in print or online related to your business. This will keep you up to date and help you to immerse yourself in the area.

Also, go and view other businesses. If you want to be a fashion designer, visit Selfridges. If you want to be a game designer, play games. If you want to be a musician, immerse yourself in music. This is not a joke. It's called *immersing yourself* and it floods your subconscious which then brings ideas back into your conscious mind for your business.

All of these tasks are easy, fun and can be done in your lunch hour, after work or in your spare time. You can even combine them with catching up with friends.

Talk to your boss

If your boss is approachable, or even as a matter of good faith, mention that you are thinking of setting up a business. Not only will it clear the air so they don't find out later and think you abused their time or your job, but they may help with support or information. I have even seen employers jump in and finance their employees in a business. Indeed, I have done this myself.

Also, your boss may give you time off to do some of the groundwork for your own business. It always pays to be upfront. The fact you are not concealing your business and putting energy into it, and telling people about what you are doing, helps to bring it about.

Marketing

I discussed marketing and the importance of promotion earlier in the book. Social media is something you can do throughout the day, although you should not spend too much time on this if you are still working full-time in another role. It can be a good way to start courting awareness of your business or publicising it in a way that takes up little time and does not cost much.

Facebook, LinkedIn, Flickr, YouTube and Twitter, can all be managed quite easily and relatively cheaply, and you can use these channels to garner awareness even before you go live with your business. You can also attract collaborators and possibly investors (particularly through LinkedIn).

Social media is a platform which makes communications easier and if you have less time then managing that time through improved communications is a great way to ensure you still can start or grow your business while you are working in another job.

Compliance

If you are working in a job and earning money from your business, even if it seems like a small amount, ensure you are set up properly for tax. If you are a PAYE earner and also self-employed or operating a company, your affairs become a little more complex and you need to ensure everything is handled correctly.

Take advice from an accountant, visit the HMRC website (**www.hmrc.gov.uk**) and undertake research to ensure you are:

- Set up tax efficiently
- Registered for VAT (if you need to be)
- Paying the correct tax

As soon as you are earning from any business, you need to register with HMRC. You can register as a partnership, limited company or as self-employed, as I outlined earlier.

If you are self-employed and plan to earn personally (as opposed to setting up your business through another structure), this, combined with the salary from your job, will increase your individual tax liability. If you are combining the business with a job, register with HMRC (**www.hmrc.gov.uk/forms/cwf1.pdf**).

Also, make sure you keep track of any expenses you incur in setting up your new business, including travelling to trade shows, buying books or registering on paid websites. These will be classified as expenses for your business's profit and loss, and can be offset against future profits. They are part of the set-up costs I talked about earlier.

Legal and moral considerations

Make sure you do not take any information from your employer to use for your own business. I'm not talking only about information you learn, but anything soft or hard that is actually owned by your employer – taking information is easy to do inadvertently.

If your boss gives you something or allows you to use it that is great, but make sure there is a paper trail and a signed document that it has been given to you legitimately. Otherwise keep your personal information and work information separate.

Check on contractual matters

A lot of start up entrepreneurs are not in part-time jobs, but may have already had a long career, maybe in the civil service, the armed forces or even in private enterprise. This is a different situation. In this case, you will need to check your contract to ensure you are allowed to work on another project, as some contracts preclude moonlighting. If you leave and sign a departure agreement, such as a termination agreement or a redundancy agreement, check that you are not subject to any restrictions after you leave.

It is certainly liberating for many people in these positions to be starting businesses and the process doesn't change. The only thing that changes is the way you go about the time sharing – communication with your boss and other stakeholders is important.

If you are going to be talking about your new business on Facebook, for example, and you are still an employee in a private company, you need to manage the stakeholders and tell them first so they don't get annoyed if the first they hear of your intentions is via social media. In the worst case scenario they could take legal action against you.

Keep an eye out

People you meet in your job can be amazingly helpful for you when starting up your own business. The boss can be helpful, but it is amazing how even your customers and clients may embrace your business and believe in you.

I am not suggesting you poach employees or steal clients. I'm saying that you should be open and honest about starting your business and operate as morally as you can. Keep an eye out for people who may gravitate towards you, who may wish to be engaged with you, work with you or buy from you.

DOING IT FROM YOUR SPARE ROOM

Whether you are holding down a day job, transitioning from a long-term job, or working only on your start up business, you may decide you do not need an office but prefer to set it up from home. This is very common and in fact is a good idea, but of course all of us have different living arrangements.

Starting and running a business is a serious undertaking and whilst it can be done from home, some boundaries and lifestyle choices are important in order to ensure you achieve maximum efficiency and output.

If you are working from home, here are some points to remember. There are likely to be many distractions so you need to have self-discipline.

Visit the British Insurance Brokers' Association (**www.biba.org.uk**) to find a broker who can advise you on this very specialised area.

Looking after employees in the workplace

This is what Paul Manley says about looking after employees in the workplace.

There are four main factors involved.

1. The welfare of your employees.
2. Minimising your legal position by listening to employees and reacting positively to their concerns.
3. Objective assessment of employee symptoms and work practices.
4. The cost of supplying equipment versus the costs of litigation.

If you think workstation injuries are not big business, note that Paul says the cost of lost production in the UK each year due to work related musculoskeletal injuries is £6bn. Many of these injuries are ultimately preventable.

He goes on to say that there are a number of reasons why routine appraisal of employees' physical state has significant benefits for businesses:

- Remedial actions can improve comfort and therefore improve productivity.
- Education empowers individuals to improve their workplace hazards and habits.
- Early identification of symptoms may help reduce long-term cumulative damage, potentially reducing lost time and financial impact on the employer.
- Reduced time off work should offset any costs of equipment required for programme implementation.
- A record of actions will provide an audit trail and assist you if you are involved with legal action or compensation claims at a later date.

8. Be comfortable

Have you ever noticed how you feel more powerful when on a call if you stand up? If not, try it.

Have you ever noticed how altering your vocal tone can change the way the person you speaking to receives your message? Try varying your voice; it's a business and communication tool.

Finally, have you ever noticed how having a sore body hampers your ability to do your work?

If you are starting up your business and are the main person, it's not like an office where you can take the day off and rest your body. Even if you take the day off, you will be thinking about work, as this is a small business person's life.

I have weekly massage treatments and I never go more than an hour at my desk without walking around the neighbourhood. I walk to and from meetings and exercise each day. I'm not holding myself up as the Hulk Hogan of the business world, just suggesting what I have found to work for me.

Everyone needs to find what works best for them. Not just now, but to keep your body in business-ready shape so that you don't get felled by problem after problem later on.

Paul Manley has the following advice on how to be comfortable. Companies and creative entrepreneurs pay Paul a lot of money for this advice, so I strongly suggest you follow it.

- When sitting, the posture that creates the least pressure on the back is when the angle at the hips and knees is about 120 degrees. Note that this is the general posture when sitting in a car, in contrast to that of the traditional office chair. Personally, though, I would say that there is still some value in the *90-90-90 rule* (which says that the angles at your hips, knees and ankles should all be 90 degrees). It is an easy rule to remember and it can help you to avoid some extreme postures. The way to think about it is that the rule can help you get into a starting position from which you can vary.

- There is no single correct posture for an eight-hour day. You must move and change positions as well as stretch and have proper furniture and equipment to keep muscles from being constantly tense. In all events, the primary goal is to stop furniture from forcing you to sit in any one awkward position.

- Leaning on a chair backrest reduces pressure on the lower back. You can optimise your position if you tilt the chair seat or by angling the back rest so that you maintain a semi-crouch position. There is nothing wrong with leaning back, as long as you are not slouching forwards from the mid-back.

- Arm rests that adequately support the weight of the arm reduce lower back stress (not merely shoulder stress).

- The classic typing posture creates the most pressure on the lower back.

MAKING THE BREAK - GOING IT ALONE

The point will come when, like a child leaving home, you know the time is right to leave your full-time job to work exclusively on your new business. Or, if you are working from home, to take your start up to the next level, which may involve more time outside the house.

How will I know the time is right?

If you are working full-time or part-time and are a *5 to 9* start up – a phrase coined by Emma Jones of Enterprise Nation – then your business will at some point grow to a critical mass at which point you will have to leave your job. This doesn't always mean your business will already have become profitable. In fact you may need to work on your start up full-time in the lead up to fund raising.

If your business is a profitable hobby on the side, it is fine for it to stay that way. However, if you intend to expand your business from *start up* to *grown up* then with growth comes change and transition. You will know, depending on your business plan and your research, when the time has come for you to leave your job.

It is important to ensure your business plan is realistic. I'm not talking about the predictions of what might happen in year three or five, as these are usually inaccurate. I mean to make sure you know what your plan is for the next year, what your cash flow is and that you have put into place all of the organisational tools mentioned in this book. Then you are ready to strike – and leave your job.

Bear in mind there are some businesses that can be run whilst you are working. However, when you want to grow, scale and particularly fundraise you will really need to be dedicated to the business rather than only providing it part of your time.

Also, for many making the break this can mean something different. It can mean actually having the courage to start a business at all – even whilst still having a job. To these creative entrepreneurs I say – read the book, take the plunge and just do it!

WHAT DO I DO AND HOW DO I DO IT?

I want to take a look at the various areas within the creative sector and see how and when you might be able to go it alone from a practical perspective.

Many creative sector entrepreneurs earn revenue on a *fee for service* basis. If you are a musician, a performer or a videographer, you are earning fees for your time. If you are an artist, a craft maker, a designer, an advertising guru or a game designer, you are more product-based. Knowing what type of revenue earner you are is important because it tells you how to approach going it alone.

A fee-for-service videographer

Fee for service revenue earners can go it alone as soon as they have an adequate regular clientele. Let's take a videographer as an example. They can of course get a day job, and I would suggest that their day job be in a production house or something else related to their field.

The videographer may start in business by filming weddings at weekends. Sooner or later, they will give their business card out and start to get enquiries from others who have seen them at weddings or those who have seen their videos and like their work. They may start doing Bar Mitzvahs, christenings, birthdays, etc.

Hopefully they will have so many commitments and so far in advance (with upfront deposits) that they feel sufficiently secure to go into business. This is not a precise science, it's just something the individual can assess when it is right for them.

Talking to your family and friends usually results in them advising you to stick with your day job, so it's worth speaking to a mentor or an objective friend you can trust to give good, straight advice.

A product-based game or app designer

Let's look at a game or app designer. They may already have a job doing just that – designing games and apps for a developer or production house. For them to go it alone they can do one of two things:

1. Set up their own consultancy.

2. Invent a game or app, get the IP protected and devise a business model, revenue stream and start fundraising.

This is clearly a more complex process than going it alone in a fee-for-service environment.

Advertising and media

Someone in advertising and media would hopefully already be working in a media agency or production house and see that they can do something differently.

To go it alone they can:

1. Leave and trust that some clients will follow them. Hopefully they can underwrite their overheads whilst they grow the business.

2. Get other agents to jointlyset up a new ad or media house and each party can bring one client from somewhere, creating immediate revenue for the new business.

3. Set up as a consultant, maybe in their own agency or alternatively working with another company in a specialised area, e.g. media buying. Many small agencies do not have all the skills they need in-house so they might contract-in skills such as media buyers. You can make a consultancy business out of this kind of area.

The situation is similar for someone in *architecture or design* wanting to start up a business.

Arts and crafts

An arts and crafter can start making products at home and at the same time hold down a job, hopefully in arts and crafts, creative design or retail. They can make immediate use of websites which sell arts and crafts, for example:

- www.etsy.com
- www.folksy.com
- www.glasgowcraftmafia.com
- www.notmassproduced.com
- www.notonthehighstreet.com
- www.shophandmade.co.uk
- www.vintagefair.co.uk

This allows them to make sales and still receive a regular income. They can make their products in their own time outside work hours, but if their sales are successful they will duly reach a stage where in order to meet demand they need to be making more and more items, which will take time. Then they can decide if they have the courage to go it alone. This is the key time for art and craft business.

Fashion design

A fashion designer will, in an ideal world, already be working in design or a retail fashion house. They may harbour dreams of opening their own store whether physical or online.

The fashion designer can follow a similar path to that of the art and craft entrepreneurs. They can of course also set up their own website, Facebook page, etc.

Setting up a fashion business requires a decision early on as to whether it is going to be a big business or a *5 to 9* evening business. The reason for this is if you are going to open a store or a proper e-commerce website there will be investment required and it will always be in a very competitive environment. So you need to assess this during the research phase and act accordingly with regard to business plans and fundraising.

Another route is to go to the Centre for Fashion Enterprise in London. You may qualify for the funding and mentoring opportunities they provide to launch your design business.

Fashion designers should start making their products and wholesale them first. This is the most risk-averse way of expanding and getting ready to go it alone because, like arts and crafts entrepreneurs, they can assess through forward orders the number and style of clients and therefore the likely revenues if they were to go full-time.

Music and performing arts

If you are a musician in the performing arts or want to be in film, TV or radio then there are myriad business opportunities you can undertake.

Depending on your skill set, and whether you are behind or in front of the camera, you can immediately start out as a freelancer. Unless you come up with a TV format or a film script, for example, the most likely business in this area of the creative sector would be as a freelancer.

In order to undertake this as a sole trader it is best to get an agent who can source jobs for you. To find an appropriate agent and get information about this sector and its opportunities, join Actors' Equity (**www.actorsequity.org**).

Publishing and e-publishing

If you want to be an author, write a manuscript and send it to various publishers. If you get a publisher to take your manuscript, the advance is unlikely to be sufficient to allow you to write full-time, but do the first book, do it well and then take it from there.

Also look at other angles like e-publishing. It is amazing how many people turn this into a viable revenue stream. Simply set up a blog, start blogging about your topic and seek followers. Once you have an audience try to attract advertisers and if successful in this you should be able to start generating revenue and profit as a full-time business.

Some famous blogs include:

- The Huffington Post News, now a multimillion dollar business with a UK office (**www.huffingtonpost.com**)
- Entertainment gossip site TMZ (**www.tmz.com**)
- Social networking blog Mashable (**www.mashable.com**)

*

Take this practical advice and use it to start your own business, then to scale and grow as soon as you can.

You don't have to be overly complex when going it alone – you can take the first step in a manageable way which acts as a transition to a bigger future game plan. Or it can be the final stop – a simple and happy way of running a business doing something you are passionate about.

SOME INSPIRATION

I mentioned earlier my involvement on the steering committee of NACUE/Create. This is a wonderful organisation to be engaged with because it is truly inspiring to see university students creating real and viable businesses.

The best part about the students is they don't have any of the educated negativity that develops in some more jaded businesspeople later in their careers.

Here are case studies on a couple of NACUE's best university and college creative sector entrepreneurs.

DASH magazine

DASH is a London-based illustrated magazine on fashion and fashion art. Published biannually and distributed worldwide, *DASH* is aimed at opinion formers with an interest in fashion and art-related fields. It has a strong focus on fashion illustration – a previously underappreciated art form currently celebrating a vivid comeback – which gives the magazine its USP.

Visually unique and with in-depth editorial content, *DASH* provides seasonal coverage and a launch platform for emerging talent from the fields of illustration, photography, the arts and journalism to showcase, and thus gain exposure, for their work.

The concept

- Biannual fashion print
- Focus on fashion illustration and fashion art
- 25,000 copies
- Distributed worldwide

DASH is run by a highly-skilled, international team and stocked internationally. It was founded and is headed up by award winning editor-in-chief, NoéMie Schwaller, edited by Harald Weiler and art and graphic direction is by Anouk Rehorek.

DASH is a creative platform to express opinions, question modern cultural values and the futility of art, without being overly didactic. The key to the magazine's contents are fashion, people and lifestyle, documented or fictitious, but never predictable. All editorial is delivered with a personal take on life and society and a defined sense of style.

Vision

DASH has found its unique creative voice far apart from the usual fashion glossies, focusing on emerging talent while paying tribute to traditional yet topical fashion trends.

It strives to deliver an overall aesthetic experience, catering to lifestyle needs of readers. Artists' visual fantasy is given free reign, so they can convey a far more potent and personal message. *DASH* finds beauty in the process itself, in fashion, art and creation.

Nomoi

What is the reason the company exists?

Nomoi builds highly functional apparel for men that makes them look and feel great.

The motivation is to place the individual at the centre of the design process, assess his daily demands, the equipment he uses, the environment he operates in, and the interactions between all of these elements.

Inspiration

The roots are in British street culture, vintage sportswear, military uniforms and suits of armour – Nomoi creates crafted apparel for the modern man.

The brand vision

The brand is different from any other as it considers the science of ergonomics. This is concerned with the fit between people, their work and their environment. From a fascination with human movement the end user is put first, taking into account their capabilities and everyday activities.

The aim is to work closely with textile manufacturers to select high-quality, durable materials in order to maximise the performance of products.

What the brand stands for

Nomoi stands for individuals who share their enthusiasm to be active and dynamic. Nomoi apparel is intended to look good and feel good.

Unique selling point (USP)

The majority of lifestyle brands focus on producing fashionable products with function coming as an afterthought, if at all. By putting function at the heart of the design process, Nomoi differentiates itself from the competition through providing clothing that encourages movement and comfort. It creates products that are both aesthetically appealing and highly functional.

The product will appeal primarily to a fashion-minded consumer; however the performance materials and ergonomic design will also attract those who are concerned with functionality over fashion.

By mapping competitors on price, style and functionality, Nomoi has identified its product USP as a combination of:

- Ergonomic design
- Progressive design detail
- Proven utility shapes and technological performance fabrics

Sounds like great clothes to work from home in!

*

These are incredible businesses and it is even more impressive that they were established by university students.

Showbizworks

Showbizworks is a London-based online entertainment agency for corporate, live, cabaret, casino and wedding entertainment.

Showbizworks operates on behalf of its clients to source and book celebrity talent and famous name musicians, often referred to as named artistes.

Their celebrity database has over 2000 names and they deal with the artistes direct, or their management.

www.showbizworks.com

CHAPTER 8

FAMOUS BRITISH SUCCESS STORIES

AS I MENTIONED EARLIER, MODELLING OTHERS is about looking at the things they did to get them where they are and the mistakes they overcame.

If you look at some of Britain's most successful creative sector entrepreneurs, you will see that they all are still actively involved in their creative art and have managed to combine this with turning their passion into a massively successful business.

These successful entrepreneurs are the walking representations that creativity and business do mix. This mix works best when the creative art is enhancing people's lives and bringing them something they love.

Let's have a look at some examples of these successful creative entrepreneurs.

Simon Cowell - TV producer

The man responsible for *Pop Idol, X Factor* and the *Got Talent* global franchises, Simon Cowell has turned his love for music (he was originally a record company executive) into an entrepreneurial TV, multimedia and music company.

He is known for managing every detail of the creative aspect of his productions and also sits at the helm of the empire he has created that spans many industries.

www.simoncowellonline.com

Sir James Dyson - industrial designer

James Dyson is an industrial designer who has become a global brand and successful businessman. He is something of a phenomenon.

Most famous for vacuum cleaners, hand dryers and washing machines, Sir James continues to pay attention to his art and still invents, as well as being a major manufacturer with plants abroad and running the Dyson Foundation.

www.dyson.com

Harvey Goldsmith C.B.E. - music promoter

Promoter and producer Harvey Goldsmith is one of the most influential men in the global music business. He is a promoter of rock concerts, charity events and television broadcasts.

He has produced, managed and promoted shows with most of the world's major artists, including Bob Dylan, Jeff Beck, The Rolling Stones, The Who, Bruce Springsteen, Santana, Led Zeppelin, The Eagles, Pavarotti, The Bee Gees, Jools Holland, Rod Stewart, Diana Ross, Shirley Bassey, U2, Eric Clapton, Queen, Elton John, Pink Floyd, Sting, Genesis and Cirque du Soleil, He has also been involved with The Prince's Trust, Luciano Pavarotti's farewell tour, Live 8, Nokia New Year's Eve and The Merchants of Bollywood.

Not only this, he has created a successful and sustainable business model which allows him to continue to do what he loves – promote.

www.harveygoldsmith.com

Sir Philip Green - retailer

Sir Philip is one of the world's richest men and one of Britain's most successful entrepreneurs. Instead of joining his family's successful property firm, he started as a clothing importer.

The owner of BHS and Topshop is well known for his business shrewdness and his understanding of the fashion market. This powerful combination has enabled him to create one of the world's most iconic stores (Topshop) and to expand it globally through utilising partners in most overseas markets.

www.arcadiagroup.co.uk

Nigella Lawson - homemaker, chef, author and TV personality

Nigella Lawson has utilised her homemaking and cooking abilities to create a brand and industry around herself. She has become a multimedia personality with numerous revenue streams. She still gets to do what she loves most, even though she is running a big business.

www.nigella.com

Stella McCartney - fashion designer

Stella McCartney has used her own creative abilities and business acumen to become a globally successful brand.

Having a Beatle for a father does not make people like your creations and it does not automatically make you a success. Stella McCartney is a truly talented creative person who has utilised commercial collaborations and joint ventures to assuage risk and further her brand, its commercial appeal and its creative integrity.

www.stellamccartney.com

Sir Cameron Mackintosh - theatre producer

Sir Cameron Mackintosh is the most successful theatrical producer in the world and one of Britain's richest men. He combines an extremely creative knowhow and understanding of musical theatre with the uncanny ability to make almost every show he produces commercially successful. He is responsible for *Cats*, *Miss Saigon*, *Phantom of the Opera*, *Les Misérables* and *Mary Poppins*.

Sir Cameron has created an industry out of the creative art of producing shows and formed an asset base of strong IP and hard assets as he owns many theatres in London.

www.cameronmackintosh.com

Tamara Mellon O.B.E. - accessories designer

The former chief creative officer (CCO) and co-founder of Jimmy Choo shoes, Tamara Mellon turned this show company into a global accessories brand.

Whilst being actively involved in the creative side as CCO, she managed to build the company up and diversify from shoes into handbags and accessories to such an extent that the company was bought by a major player.

Kate Moss - model

Kate Moss is a British model that has made an industry around herself.

Originally shooting to fame over 20 years ago, Kate Moss has managed her career and her image through its ups and downs commercially, such that she is now known not only as a model, but also as a businesswoman, designer and British icon. She even appeared at the Olympic Games closing ceremony in London 2012.

Elizabeth Murdoch - TV production company

Coming from a family media empire you might have expected Elizabeth Murdoch to join the business, not launch a start up. However she founded her own TV production company Shine, which has, gone on to have a global reach.

With shows such as *MasterChef*, *The Office* and *The Biggest Loser*, Shine has to become one of the most powerful and influential British-owned TV production companys.

www.shine.tv

Jamie Oliver M.B.E. - chef and TV personality

Originally a chef, Jamie Oliver has turned his passion for the creative art of cooking into an international conglomerate.

He owns restaurants both directly and through joint ventures and he has a multimedia presence, earning revenue and proliferating his brand though TV shows, books, internet forums and live shows (one of which appeared at the theatre for which I was chairman in Sydney).

www.jamieoliver.com

J.K. Rowling O.B.E. - author

A globally successful author, J.K. Rowling has not only shown herself to be an amazing writer, but is credited with getting children back into reading around the world, with her *Harry Potter* book and subsequent movie series.

Through being good at her creative art and focusing on giving the readers the good-quality books that they want, Rowling has become wealthy and has created a successful business and asset base (the IP of her work).

www.jkrowling.co.uk

Charles Saatchi - advertising

Charles Saatchi was co-founder of Saatchi & Saatchi, one of the largest and most successful advertising agencies in history, and later co-founder of M&C Saatchi. He is now an art collector and founder of the Saatchi Gallery. He is a lover of the arts, an ad-man at heart, but also a successful and wealthy entrepreneur.

www.saatchi-gallery.co.uk

Michael Acton Smith - game creator

Michael Acton Smith, founder of *Moshi Monsters*, has turned his love of computer games into a global game empire. From his base in Tech City, he supervises the global proliferation of his multimedia *Moshi Monsters* empire through his company Mind Candy.

He still loves being involved in his own game creations and now has a company creating magazines, DS video games, music albums, books and of course more games.

www.mindcandy.com

Sir Paul Smith - fashion designer

Sir Paul Smith is a globally successful clothing designer, wholesaler, retailer and franchisor.

Far from being alienated from his creative endeavours, Sir Paul is well known to be hands-on in his creations and still actively involved in design.

www.paulsmith.co.uk

Lord Webber - composer

Andrew Lloyd Webber composed the music for *Phantom of the Opera, Jesus Christ Superstar, Cats and Les Misérables.* Many of his compositions have later been produced or co-produced with Sir Cameron Mackintosh.

As well as owning the rights to many of these shows, Lloyd Webber owns many theatres in London and has offices around the world producing shows with partners under his Really Useful Group brand.

www.andrewlloydwebber.com

CHAPTER 9

WORDS OF WISDOM

I SPOKE TO SOME MAJOR PLAYERS IN BRITAIN'S enterprise sector and here is what they had to say to British creative sector entrepreneurs.

❝Go for it. Be the one who changes your industry.**❞**

Lord Jeffrey Archer

❝ There is no better place in the world than the UK to tame those two opposing forces of artistic creativity and the commercial sector. It is a tough fight but with skill, perseverance and a drop of luck you can flourish in both disciplines.**❞**

Tristan Baker, producer, _Footloose_

❝NACUE Create enables a growing community of creative entrepreneurs that would otherwise be isolated to succeed. Creativity is at the very heart of British culture and despite the lack of funding for both the arts and creative businesses, we're here to represent the thousands of young creative entrepreneurs that do want to succeed in their creative careers and contribute to both the cultural and economic British landscape.**❞**

Luka Blackman-Gibbs, founder and manager, NACUE Create

❝ Engagement with customers and users is essential – getting their feedback and input to help shape the product or service can make a real difference – which unfortunately too many teams and developers fail to do.**❞**

Jon Bradford, TechStars London

❝ Britain is renowned throughout the world for the creativity of its people; it's part of the national DNA which has influenced, led, inspired and revolutionised art, culture, theatre, dance, design, literature, film, radio, digital, fashion, architecture, games and thought across the world. Our creative industries are held in huge regard around the world and, collectively, are a major, dynamic and sustainable part of our economy. **❞**

Bernard Donoghue, director, The Association of Leading Visitor Attractions

❝ You can't worry about falling flat on your face. Don't give much time to naysayers; plunge in and just go for it. If I'd thought too long and hard about approaching Oscar-winning actor Kevin Spacey about running the Old Vic, of course I'd have never done it. I have a determination to achieve what may, on the face of it, seem like either absurdly over reaching or just plain crazy.

My advice would be to be yourself, don't mould your personality to suit others but use what you're born with. Don't over-fill your schedule but allow some breathing time so you can think creatively about an idea and then form a strategy about how to achieve it. Be your strongest advocate, work hard, stay focused and be confident! **❞**

Sally Greene, CEO, Old Vic Theatre, Criterion Theatre, Ronnie Scott's Jazz Club and Greene Light Films

❝ There's never been a better time to start a business in Britain. You can start by 'Working 5 to 9' which is the term I apply to holding onto the day job and building a business at nights and weekends, you can get going on a budget, and there's support available at every turn. What's important is to take that first step of turning your creative passion or skill into a way of making a living. Doing so will be one of the best decisions you ever take. **❞**

Emma Jones, M.B.E., CEO, Enterprise Nation, StartUp Britain

❝ The British creative sector is not only a great cultural contributor but also an economic one. The film and TV industry continues to attract entrepreneurs as there is a range of options available to those with skill and passion to really achieve success. **❞**

Pippa Lambert, CEO-ICM Agency

❝ The UK's comparative advantage in the creative industries is second to none. Our main challenge is to leverage this advantage in the emerging markets which are forecast to grow to $30 trillion by 2025 by McKinsey whilst combating the commoditization of creative IP through technology, which, while providing scale to IP generators also fragments distribution & erodes margins.

To win in emerging markets, UK creatives need to show humility, by altering their mindsets and approaches to accept that our way is not always the best and deal with the idiosycrancies of those markets, which can be done through collaboration with local partners. **❞**

Keith Moses, International Trade Adviser, UK Trade & Investment

❝ London and the UK are ideal for tech and digital economy businesses for a number of reasons, but the main two are that it has an amazing lifestyle completed by a thriving ecosystem that can support high-potential creative and digital economy businesses. When you add to that some of the best talent and strong business sectors such as ecommerce, creative media and financial services, you have the right environment to help accelerate digital economy businesses faster than other locations. **❞**

Eric Van der Kleij, Special Advisor - Fintech Canary Wharf, Former CEO - Tech City

❝ Whilst it is admirable to do your *best*, invariably it is infinitely better to do everything necessary. In order to achieve this you will need to find out what *everything necessary* entails.

Are your communication skills up to scratch? Successful people are great communicators.

Losing your temper loses the argument. Deal with confrontation immediately. Address the person or people in a calm manner so as to correct the point at issue and aim to earn their respect without pulling rank or using aggression.

If failure is on the horizon make it happen quickly and move on. However, don't consider a result in terms of success or failure but as outcome – use it all as a learning curve. **❞**

Michael Vine, entertainment entrepreneur

NEXT STEPS

DON'T FORGET THESE CRUCIAL STEPS:

1. Vision, mission and values

2. Choose the appropriate business system

3. Research

4. Avoid time-honoured mistakes

5. Set your marketing plan

6. Be aware of legal nuances and possible issues ahead

7. Have an understanding of key financial areas and ratios for your sector and sub-sector

8. Regularly practice pitching

9. Study successes and model them

10. Be aware of your own psyche and psychology. Try and master yourself at all times, to harness positive energy for success.

CONCLUDING THOUGHTS

How to become a professional business person without losing your creative streak

PASSION IS DEFINED BY THE OXFORD ENGLISH Dictionary as "a strong and barely controllable emotion". This is the emotion felt by most creative sector entrepreneurs. For these people, working becomes an obsession and sleeping under the desk or pulling all-nighters to design, code or write becomes an ordinary part of life.

In a creative business, entrepreneurs need to use their imagination for the creative part and business acumen to transition from a hobby to a commercial business. The fallacy that profit is a dirty word and that creative business is not a bona fide business has been shredded by today's business society. Creative industries have been around as a business for millennia – one look at Roman amphitheatres will tell you that.

Further to that, creative businesses add to the cultural fabric of their society and give the world an immeasurable legacy that lasts hundreds of years. Look at Mozart, Da Vinci and Shakespeare – they were all creative entrepreneurs of their day. They were savvy people who knew their market, created good products, loved what they did and delivered it in such a way that it stood the test of time.

Look at Steven Spielberg, jewellers De Beers and Laurence Graff, Charles Saatchi and British-born *Vogue* editor Anna Wintour – these are game changers in traditional creative sectors. Then examine Steve Jobs, Napster's Sean Parker and Amazon's Jeff Bezos – they are all game changers that used disruptive technology to create traditional creative sector industries.

The thing that stands out about all of these entrepreneurs is their true passion for what they do. They embody their vision and are the walking manifestation of their creative processes, but yet they have all been amazingly successful at commercialising their craft. They do not have a money obsession, but they have a crystal-clear focus for their creative passion and strong institutions backed up by research and market analysis of what the market wants and needs.

Don't forget the real-life stories of creative sector entrepreneurs outlined in the book and the students being guided by their creativity and matching that with their desire to start up and grow businesses. They have used their creative gifts to do something better than anyone else in their field.

With the creative sector accounting for 6% of UK GDP, employing around 5% of the population, and 3% of EU GDP and 3% of EU employment, you cannot argue against it being important. In light of the British government's focus on growing the creative sector, along with European cultural and creative industry in its 2020 strategy, it is impossible to advance a case for anything other than the growth of this sector as a serious business.

This is not to say that everyone who is creative should be in business. You may be happy doing it as a hobby or as an after-hours business. However, you should not be anything other than filled with encouragement, inspiration and support should you wish to start up and get into business. Being in business is liberating, free of many restrictions and allows you to be responsible for yourself. It is only risky if you don't take the right advice and fail to structure your business correctly.

Some may say business crushes your creative streak. There is no question that the minute commerciality is involved it does alter the operation somewhat. However, your best asset is you; you are the one in charge of generating creative ideas and you are more than capable of keeping on top of things as commerciality infuses these ideas. If the businesses causes you stress, frustration and irritation then manage that. Manage it emotionally, manage it by getting good advice and manage it by setting the foundations and structure from the start so it is strong. Be obsessed only by doing what you do well and having fun in the process.

As British author John Kay says in his book *Obliquity*: "Goals are best achieved when pursued indirectly." This is the perfect articulation of the reasons why you should pursue only your creative passion and meet the market need in a cost-effective manner. Do not focus on making money only, on being the best businesses person or on the day-to-day administration of running the business. Either outsource these areas that cause anxiety or, if you cannot, then compartmentalise them and have creative days and administration days.

That way, on the creative days you know you are safe to be creative only and on the business days you are aware that you only need to focus on the left-brain stuff for a limited period of time, during which time you allow yourself to have a break from being creative.

Is being an entrepreneur easier than getting a job? Well, do you think putting all your eggs in the one basket with a boss is wise? Can you be sure of his or her business acumen? Being an employee is the right path for some, but being an entrepreneur is the right path for others. There is of touch the middle ground where you can hold a job and be a *5-9 entrepreneur*, starting and operating a business after hours whilst still having the regular pay cheque coming in.

See what fits your own profile and do what your gut tells you. Don't be disappointed with yourself in, say, 20 years when you look back and think what you might have achieved if you had taken the risk. As the wise people say, in life you most regret what you don't do.

I have provided you with the key steps so that you can literally put down the book and start planning. Remember, define your vision, identify the need and then you have the tools to begin building. *Vision* and *Need*. That's where the process begins!

If you are not inspired, you are not passionate about your concept of vision. It's black and white. If you are passionate but scared about taking the leap into business, get energetic, be strong for the sake of yourself and move on it.

You may be a game-changer, you may be a mogul, but one thing is for sure, you will spend every day for the rest of your life living your dream and passion and sharing it with the world.

INDEX

checklist of ingredients for success 4-5

coach *see* mentor

combining business and day job 171-6

Companies House 28, 35

company 5, 34-5, 92-3, 174

competitive advantage 68, 84, 126, 156

  comparative advantage 84

  differential advantage 20, 84

Conran, Terence 6

contracts 71, 93-5,

  for business acquisition 53

  for your employment 175

  looking at when buying a business 50

courage 6-7, 184, 187,

Cowell, Simon 3, 6, 195

crafts 4, 6, 54, 107, 186-7

Create Wales 141

Creative Scotland 140

creative sector 3, 26, 30, 32, 76, 82, 153, 212

credit 26, 71

customers 4, 19-20, 27, 64, 71, 74, 76-8, 90, 94, 96, 178

  considering when buying a business 48, 50, 51,

Dare to Prepare 156

DASH magazine 189-90

day job, combining with business 171-6

debt-to-equity ratio 104

Dirty Dancing – The Classic Story on Stage (*Dirty*

Dancing) xiv, 23, 41, 85, 115, 129, 130

distribution 74-80, 90, 108,

Dragons' Den 121, 124, 141

due diligence 26, 46-7, 52

Duke, Mike 155-6

Dyson, Sir James 196

early career (of Michael Jacobsen) xiii-xiv

education 156, 181

Ek, Daniel 82, 86-7

Enterprise Nation 142, 183

ETSY 56

EU (European Union) xvi, 24, 153, 212

expenses 29, 69, 108-10, 111-2, 174

Facebook 27, 28, 65, 88, 173, 175

family and friends

  money from 29, 49, 64, 113

  negativity of 153-4, 185

fashion designer 107, 187

Fashion Angel 143

fee fatigue 53

fee for service xiv, 184, 185

film 41, 72, 185, 188

finance 29-32, 62, 103-12

  day-to-day tips 111-2

  raising 124-8

  ratios 103-5

  statements 105-10

fitness 157-8, 161-5